Engage
Connect
Grow

52 Lessons to help guide individuals and corporate teams
to the heart of what truly matters to them

Aaron Solly

Published by Engage Coaching Group Dec, 2016
ISBN: 9780980936827

Book Cover Design: Judith Mazari
Editor: Nina Shoroplova
Typeset: Greg Salisbury
Portrait Photographer: Wade Gibb

DISCLAIMER: This is a work of non-fiction. The information is of a general nature to help you on the subject of business and personal developement. Readers of this publication agree that neither Aaron Solly, nor his publisher will be held responsible or liable for damages that may be alleged or resulting directly or indirectly from their use of this publication. All external links are provided as a resource only and are not guaranteed to remain active for any length of time. Neither the publisher nor the author can be held accountable for the information provided by, or actions resulting from accessing these resources.

Thank you to everyone who has shown support and provided me with guidance through my own personal growth journey and the writing of this workbook. You are all bright beacons of light reminding me of my gifts and my calling to do this work.

CONTENTS

PREFACE

When I first knew I wanted to write this workbook, I had just come from an "I Can Do It" conference. I went to see Wayne Dyer and Marianne Williamson. I ended up learning something from all the speakers in attendance.

I was lying on my futon in the spare bedroom of my home at eleven o'clock at night. I don't normally spend any time in this room. For some reason, I felt compelled to do so.

Plus, it was supermoon Saturday. There was something inside me that told me to take my laptop and a cup of tea and go up to the spare room to write with the moon overlooking me through the window.

I actually didn't feel well at that moment. I had a headache and my stomach didn't feel a hundred percent. Yet, I was drawn to write something about this workbook no matter how little. I felt compelled to start writing and see what happened.

This is it. This workbook is me sharing the real me for close to forty years of my life. I have included my fears, my questions about life, my challenges, struggles, my depression, my connection to the Universe (God), my journey as a father, my schooling, my pain, my passion, and my joy.

I have to admit I am feeling nervous. It has been scary to consider sharing my journal entries with the world. People are going to read thoughts only I have shared with myself for all these years. My ego is warning me about the judgement that may occur.

Having said that, something inside me has been telling me this can help people. These are lessons. They are not to be embarrassed about. Writing this workbook is a way to help people. It's a way to help me get to where I want to be.

I grew up in an amazing family with ongoing love and support. A lot of the struggles, battles, and turmoil I faced in my life were all in my head. For me, they seemed like huge struggles.

I spent a lot of my time as a kid focusing on what was going to make me happy—to have friends, to be liked, to be accepted, and to feel included. I ran into struggles with trying to be happy as a child. I felt like I was picked on a lot of the time. It was the words that were said to me that really had an impact on me.

Those words impacted my self-esteem and who I believed I was. I took them to heart. I didn't know how to handle them.

As I grew older, I had a lot of moments when I felt lost and confused. I felt embarrassed about who I was. I tended to be quiet, shy, and reserved most of the time. I had a lot of acne in high school and tried all the medications to try to relieve it. This feeling of not being normal carried on into university, by when I thought it would have disappeared.

When I entered university, I started to write. I wrote about the thoughts in my head. I wrote about the questions I had. I wrote about the dreams I had.

I tried to get on paper what was going on in my head. I wrote poems. I wrote as best I could about what was going on for me. The thoughts were primarily negative ones; they seemed to play over and over again in my head.

I started to notice that it felt good to write out my thoughts. I used the process to express anger as I didn't normally feel comfortable expressing anger openly. I believed that being angry was a bad thing. I expressed it through writing words and even scribbling.

It was confusing to me that I had these emotions coming up. What was it about me that I was dealing with things this way when everyone else seemed fine and not worried about the same things I worried about? What was wrong with me? No one else seemed to be struggling with these things.

I spent a lot of my life in my head. I believed I had to plan everything I was going to say in advance. I wanted to control things so as to not look stupid and attract attention to myself. There were times when I had a whole different world going on in my head about what people thought about me. I also imagined expressing myself in the way that I actually wanted to, but I never had the courage to do it for real.

In my late twenties, I was diagnosed with depression. I would have periods of time when I was in a grey fog and it felt as though no light was coming in. Everything seemed too hard—a constant struggle. Getting out of bed was a struggle. Trying to plan a few days in advance seemed impossible.

I would write about it. I would get on paper anything that came to me. I hoped that one day soon the light would come back into my life again. I wanted to feel better. I was pretty hard on myself for feeling down. Ultimately, I was searching for answers to feel better. I wanted so badly to feel better.

It took me many years of focusing on the outside world to realize that approach was not working. When I focused on the outside world, I found proof for the negative beliefs I had about myself.

Journaling has been one way I have been able to gradually stop focusing outside myself. What I have come to understand is my journaling has been a way of taking care of myself and becoming more engaged with whom I am. It has enabled me to increase my engagement as an employee, a partner, and a father.

Journaling has been a powerful tool that has helped me to get through what I felt were tough times in my life and to answer important questions about life. It also has helped me write about those moments when I felt amazing, on track with my life, inspired, and connected with who I am.

I do want to commend you for reading this workbook. You may be at a time in your life when you are seeking a different way of getting what you truly want. There is no mistake that you are reading this workbook. Mistakes do not exist.

I have had many books and resources come into my life and I still do today. This happened at certain points in my life when I needed help. I believe we are called to find our teachers when we need them.

My hope is this workbook will get you closer to where you want to be and bring some heightened awareness to your own situation.

I am here right now to tell you that your life can be better. In fact, it is better. It may be possible that your vision is blurred by the struggles you face in your life right now.

There is a way through the darkness, the struggle, and the fear.

in addition to the support I received from family, friends, and therapists, journaling became one of the ways that guided me through my darkness, struggles, and fears.

You are full of love, light, and happiness. They are infinite. They live inside you. It took me many years to start to understand this.

It is not something we have to find outside of ourselves. This is a very powerful thing to know. You are in complete control of your life. You have the power to be happy, to feel love, and to live the life you absolutely and completely desire.

Much love, hugs, and compassion to you.

Aaron Solly

INTRODUCTION

ARE YOU READY TO CHANGE YOUR LIFE?

Is now the time to get real about changing your life?

Have you been thinking about all the ways you want to improve your life and yet hesitated to take the next steps?

Are you feeling discouraged at work and seeking a new way to feel excited and inspired in your job?

There are so many things that can cause us to not stay focused on our goals, dreams, and passions in life.

The process of determining and clearly defining our goals can limit this focus. The way we were brought up and the lessons we were taught impact us. The daily thoughts running through our heads can be majorly distracting. The beliefs we have about ourselves can create a constant block holding us back.

There are many factors that directly impact our ability to make real change in our personal life and our career.

I know this because I have experienced them myself, struggling with worry negative thoughts for many years. I would have moments of believing in myself and then periods when I lacked any confidence in my abilities.

Depression was a regular occurrence in my life. It took me many years to shift my relationship to it and to better understand why I was experiencing it.

I started journaling in 1992 when I was at university. I continued using journaling into my adult years and it became a tremendous tool to help me start to ask the big questions I had about my life. Initially, these were questions I was afraid to ask others.

In this workbook, I share some of my own journal entries to help show the personal transformation journaling initiated for me.

This workbook is going to teach you to use the tool of journaling. It will show you that something as simple as putting words on paper can bring about clarity, creativity, connection, and growth.

JOURNALING CAN HELP YOU CHANGE YOUR LIFE

An article published by Michael Grothaus in FastCompany.com entitled, "Why Journaling Is Good For Your Health (And 8 Tips To Get Better)" highlights the health benefits from journaling.

The article mentions research by Dr. James Pennebaker, who is a psychologist and leading expert in a field he created, something, he calls "Expressive Writing." Pennebaker finds that journaling strengthens immune cells, lowers levels of depression and anxiety, and increases positive mood, social engagement, and the quality of relationships.

The University of Rochester Medical Center finds journaling can improve mental health. The benefits include managing anxiety, reducing stress, and coping with depression, to name a few.

THE WORKPLACE NEEDS HELP

The data in North America and worldwide shows a decline in employee engagement in the workplace. These recent percentages offered by Gallup really jumped out at me.

"70% of U.S. workers not engaged at work" ("State of the American Workplace report Feb 2017")

U.S. Employees—Not engaged 51%; Actively disengaged 16% ("Workplace Disruption: From Annual Reviews to Coaching" February 2017)

Engaged Employees Worldwide 13% ("Can Bad Managers Be Saved?" December 2016)

There is a tremendous opportunity to bring more personal development tools and resources to the workplace. People are at work more hours of their life than they are at home. The productivity during these hours can be greatly impacted if the mental state of the employees is weak.

I have written this workbook to help employees, corporate teams, and organization become more engaged and connected to obtain growth.

A key method of increasing employee engagement is through journaling and ongoing support.

This workbook is a guided method for you personally and for a group to commit to change and improvement together.

As the member of a team or a group, you will be given the opportunity to use these lessons to truly get to know your coworkers. The idea is to connect team members because through this connection growth can occur. This growth may result in achievement in areas the team never thought of before.

There are 52 lessons in this workbook, divided into three sections: Engage, Connect, Grow. One way to work through the workbook is to complete one exercise per week. This is recommended as the exercises are meant to create a foundation of awareness and learning along the way.

Having said that, you or your team may want to focus on connecting first, if this is an area of focus. Or, if you have done a lot of work related to engaging and connecting already and would like to look at specific ways to improve growth personally and as part of a team, you can jump to the section entitled "Grow."

You may notice I use italics in some of my journaling entries. I use them to highlight the response I received when I asked a question. For example, the journal entry I include in lesson 13 involves a written conversation I had with my depression to get a better understanding of my relationship to it.

You can use this workbook in whatever way will benefit you to achieve your goals and make the needed improvements to attain more connection and growth.

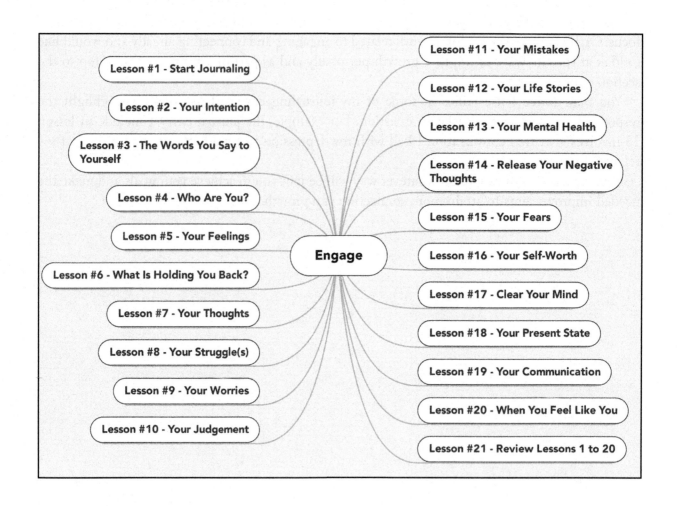

Part #1
ENGAGE

"Everyone enjoys doing the kind of work for which he is best suited." Napoleon Hill

The definition of "to engage" is "to participate or become involved."

This section of the workbook gives you the opportunity to become more engaged in your life, your work, your team, and so on.

It is time to wake up to what is really going on and what has being going for perhaps some time.

I will give you exercises to help you become more aware of areas such as your intention, the thoughts you have, your judgements, and your feelings.

This is the foundational section of the workbook. Its focus will guide you into areas of your life that are core to your challenges and can explain why you are where you are at this time in your life. The exercises are simple and easy to complete. You can go as deeply into the exercises as you wish.

I invite you to receive each lesson with openness and curiosity. Ultimately, you get to decide how much work you want to invest in improving yourself and your life.

Lesson # 1
START JOURNALING

Over the years, the things I wrote about and the way I wrote about them changed a lot. Ultimately, I just started writing back in the 1990s and things have evolved over time.

Some ways to get started could be the following:

- What happened yesterday or today that stands out?
- What is something you are struggling with?
- What are you looking forward to?
- What is something you would like to improve in your life?

Here is an example of one of my journal entries from the 1990s. On this day I decided to write all the things about myself I was not happy with.

JOURNAL ENTRY IN 1990S

Focus too much on material things – "What's New!"

Learn passively

Becoming too much individualistic

Not being rational with decisions I make

Relying on others' opinions before determining my own

Not communicating my thoughts, feelings, ideas effectively

Not conscious of what others think or say

Intimidated by those of high education or popularity

Trying to satisfy everyone and forgetting about myself

Rely too much on others—follower

Weak, always in need of someone

Not focusing on goals enough

Need to be more open and direct with people

Too shy

Get uncomfortable very easily

Nervousness and worrier about future

Must live in the now or nothing will ever happen in my life

Talk more about other people or things rather than myself

A different life in my head; see how I want to be seen by people

How to act or talk

Too wrapped up in this image that I can't be who I am

I don't know who I am

Trying to be someone I am not

Have trouble speaking up or talking with people

Make situation uncomfortable

Don't intro myself or friends right away

Determining how I feel, what I think, I agree with everything

Seems like everyone knows more than me

I don't know a lot about anything in great detail

Know things in general not specifics

Afraid to speak up

Scared about what people think of me

Act how others expect rather than what's "natural"

JOURNAL ENTRY IN 2014

Let's move forward about fourteen years. Here is what I wrote in my journal on April 25, 2014 at 1:00 a.m.

I love you. I love you, Aaron Solly. I love you.

I love you. You are love. You deserve it.

You follow it. You get it.

EXERCISE FOR YOU

Try it. Start today. Write anything. Actually, you can draw it, paint it, record it, sing it, dance it if you prefer. There no limits to your journaling. You can use it in whatever way allows you to connect with yourself. There are only right ways to do this.

A great place to start is to write about things you have done today or things you saw on your way to work.

_____

_____

_____

_____

EXERCISE FOR YOUR TEAM OR GROUP

Have the team members share what they wrote from the individual exercise.

_____

_____

_____

_____

Break the team into groups to write something creative together within fifteen minutes. Then you have each group share what they wrote.

_____

_____

_____

_____

Lesson # 2

YOUR INTENTION

It has taken me many years to fully understand how to articulate my intention.

Over the years, I have learned my goal or intention should be experience-based. What does it feel like, look like, sound like? It should not be a thing, such as a material object. It should be focused on ultimately what I am seeking by having the material object.

Your intention will always be something you can come back to especially when struggles arise and also when decisions need to be made.

You can remember where you want your focus to be and bring your attention there versus focusing on fear.

Below you can read two very different journals entries and see the transition of my own intention.

This is a journal entry I wrote related to what I wanted in 1998.

JOURNAL ENTRY FROM 1998

I want to be recognized,
I want to be heard,
Can you see me? I'm over here.
I want to be recognized,
I want to be heard,
I want to be recognized
and seen all over the world.
I want to be recognized,
I want to be seen,
How hard can it be?
What do I need to prove?
How long does it take?
I don't want to have to wait.

I can see my reflection, so I am for real,

Maybe I don't want to be recognized,

Maybe I already have been, By me.

The waiting should end for I have been recognized by the most important person of all, myself.

JOURNAL ENTRY FROM 2014

Here is another journal entry about my intention sixteen years later.

April 25, 2014, 9:14 p.m.

What do I want?

My intention is to open my soul, mind, & body

to what it is I truly want.

Rest

Peace

Joy

Loving relationship

Family

Authenticity

Solid

Openness

Unconditional love

Freedom

EXERCISE FOR YOU

You can start writing about your intention by writing what you want. Next write about what you will be feeling and experiencing if you get what you want. Write that feeling and experience as your intention or goal. Describe your goal or intention in a few words or a short sentence. Focus on the experience you want to have versus the thing itself, for example, "Peace and Joy" versus "Travelling to an exotic place."

What is the thing you actually want in your life?

_____

_____

_____

_____

What will you be feeling and experiencing if you get what you want?

_____

_____

_____

_____

Describe your goal or intention.

_____

_____

_____

_____

What would you experience if you accomplished your intention?

_____

_____

_____

_____

What does it feel like, look like, sound like?

_____

_____

_____

_____

EXERCISE FOR YOUR TEAM OR GROUP

You can have the team members share their personal goal or intention if people are open to it. Write out what they share.

_____

_____

_____

_____

Describe the team goal or intention in a few words or short sentence. Focus on the experience the team wants to have versus the thing itself.

_____

_____

_____

_____

Have a discussion about what this team or group actually wants to accomplish.

_____

_____

_____

_____

What does the intention feel like, look like, sound like?

_____

_____

_____

_____

What would the team or group experience if the intention were accomplished?

_____

_____

_____

_____

Lesson # 3

THE WORDS YOU SAY TO YOURSELF

What are you saying to yourself throughout any given day? The words you say to yourself can have a great impact on how you make decisions in your life. They can impact how you feel and how you interact with your family and the people at your work.

Below, you can read a couple of journal entries I wrote regarding this.

JOURNAL ENTRY JANUARY 12, 2000

I have been noticing that I do tend to take people's reactions the wrong way. I normally don't say hi to someone unless they look at me and I think I feel slightly rejected by people who don't go out of their way to say hi. I feel like I'm not important. I'm a loser. I put their words in my head.

JOURNAL ENTRY MARCH 4, 2014

Life is a maze & love is a riddle.
Bring me peace.
Bring me peace.
I want peace.
How can we feel Peace now?

EXERCISE FOR YOU

Spend this week really noticing the words you say to yourself. This is an exercise you may find helpful to do regularly to get a true sense of the impact the words you use have on your self-esteem and confidence. You may want to keep your journal with you so you can write your thoughts down when you notice them.

Write what you are saying to yourself.

_____

_____

_____

_____

Are there words you use on a regular basis?

_____

_____

_____

_____

Are there labels or names your call yourself?

_____

_____

_____

_____

What do you say to yourself when you make a mistake?

_____

_____

_____

_____

What do you say to yourself when you achieve a goal?

_____

_____

_____

_____

EXERCISE FOR YOUR TEAM OR GROUP

Discuss what the group members say to themselves about your team or group, if people are open to this.

_____

_____

_____

_____

Are there words the team or team members use to describe the group?

_____

_____

_____

_____

Are there labels each of you calls the team or group?

_____

_____

_____

_____

What happens when the team makes a mistake?

_____

_____

_____

_____

What do you say about your team or group when one of you or all of you achieve a goal?

_____

_____

_____

_____

NOTES

Lesson # 4

WHO ARE YOU?

Who are you really? Do you find yourself questioning this?
Here is a journal entry of mine from the mid-1990s when I was questioning who I was.

JOURNAL ENTRY MID-1990S

I lie here wide awake thinking,
Thoughts of the future and what it holds,
Seems to be following a straight line with no curve in sight,
Where's my curve?
I'd enjoy doing something out of the ordinary,
Something unpredicted and spontaneous.
Thinking along a straight line has made me shallow,
Unable to branch out to new and better things.
Am I scared? Probably, why?
Doing the different [thing] is something new,
Meaning a change, an unnatural change.
Who is to change me, myself?
What can't I break away from the daily routine,
Venture out to find a more fulfilling life?
Is there anything wrong with my life now?
I want to do with my life, no nothing is wrong.
Why do I always worry?
Worrying about the future, what people think, what people say.
What about what I think and what I say?
Expressions, I would not necessarily know in my vocab.
What is that? Scared, worried again?

Time to break away, feel alive, be me,
Who am I?
Why do I question this?
Should I know who I am?
Better than anyone else.
Time for bed.

JOURNAL ENTRY JANUARY 25, 2001

Below are some journal entries—from 2001, 2007, and 2013. You may notice I found more clarity over time about who I am.

There are many colours in my life right now,
There are colours that are bright and refreshing,
They are colours that are relaxing and soothing,
They are fun and make me laugh,
They are part of my life and I am glad,
These colours seem to be expanding from time to time,
They are becoming more common around me, everywhere I am,
They are doing too much for me these colours,
They are controlling things with their shimmer and glow,
They do not realize that they don't have to be in control,
They can let others' colours take on the battle,
They are friendly, but smart,
They are clever and can be manipulated without realizing it,
They can be orange one day and blue the next day.
I am confident, I am bold,
My life will make sense when I am old,
Goals are important I see that now,
My brain seems tired, it's hard to say how much info it will allow,
Living everyday like it's your last is hard to do when you are not having a blast,
Finding true love is what everyone wants,

You can write her a letter in all sorts of fonts,

Then raising a fam that's not easy today,

Work all day all night for an honest pay,

Life in general seems quite simple,

It's the day to day that causes the pimples,

Don't sweat the small stuff and all will be good,

Give me a vacuum to clear my mind and then I could,

It's those that you bring with you along the way that make the difference,

Friends and family give you strength and they give you guidance

Remember this even if it doesn't rhyme.

Your mind will be clear, your heart will be strong, you will be fine.

JOURNAL ENTRY OCTOBER 17, 2007

Why am I here?

To help people:

LOVE MORE

SAVE MORE

EXCEL MORE

RESPECT MORE

PLAY MORE

LAUGH MORE

BREATHE MORE

LIVE MORE

EDUCATE OTHERS ABOUT HOW TO GET WHAT LIFE IS REALLY ABOUT

EXERCISE FOR YOU

Spend some time writing about anything related to who you are.
Who are you?

_____

_____

_____

_____

What are your fears, your doubts, your excitement, your feelings, and your talents?

_____

_____

_____

_____

What makes you who you are?

_____

_____

_____

_____

What have you accomplished?

_____

_____

_____

_____

What are you afraid of?

_____

_____

_____

_____

What do you call yourself?

_____

_____

_____

_____

What excites you?

_____

_____

_____

_____

What are your talents?

_____

_____

_____

_____

EXERCISE FOR YOUR TEAM OR GROUP

Who is the team or group?

_____

_____

_____

_____

What makes your team or group who it is?

_____

_____

_____

_____

What have you accomplished as a team or group?

_____

_____

_____

_____

What is the team or group afraid of?

_____

_____

_____

_____

What does the team or group call itself?

_____

_____

_____

_____

What excites the team or group?

_____

_____

_____

_____

What are the talents of the team or group?

_____

_____

_____

_____

Lesson # 5

YOUR FEELINGS

It took me many years to realize the power of actually feeling my feelings. I used to avoid them. I avoided them to the point where I didn't really know how to deal with them. I held on to anger. I believed that happiness was the only feeling to focus on. I thought if I wasn't happy, there must be something wrong with me.

Here is a journal entry from 2000 about me expressing my feelings.

JOURNAL ENTRY MARCH 19, 2000

I'm feeling isolated. I don't know if that's the word, but I don't feel like talking to anybody. It's like someone could say whatever they wanted to me & I would just sit there not replying. Little things have been frustrating me. It's like I just want to hide in my room for a while. My self-esteem has depleted & I don't know why. This seems to happen every few months.

JOURNAL ENTRY FEBRUARY 23, 2012

You may notice in this journal entry how my relationship with my feelings has evolved and changed.

Thank you for your love today! I witnessed it in a variety of ways. The cat is showing me love right now. bless you. Love you.

I got to feel and it was painful.
I got to feel and it was scary.
I got to feel and it was wonderful.

I got to feel.
I got to feel.

I got to feel and it woke me up.
I got to feel and it cleared my head.
I got to feel and it made me laugh.

I got to feel.
I got to feel.

I got to feel and share it with the world.
I got to feel and it gave me a voice.
I got to feel and it scared those around me.

I got to feel.
I got to feel.

I got to feel & now it is in hiding.
I got to feel & the fear is on.
I got to feel & I have moments that I have lost it.

I got to feel.
I got to feel.

I feel the anxiety & fear,
I feel strength I didn't have before,
I feel lighter & clearer,
I feel I can do this,
I feel a new sense of love surrounding me,
I feel grateful, so grateful,
I feel comforted that even if I don't feel this 100% it is ok.

JOURNAL ENTRY OCTOBER 2013

Hello, sadness, tell me about you.

I am awake. I have been asleep.

I want to exist as part of you.

I am a part of you. I am here to teach and to heal.

It is okay to feel sad.

With sadness comes an awakening, breakthroughs and you.

You deserve joy so feel sad. Really feel it.

You are sad about loss. It is ok. Why are you sad?

Hold on to it. let it be.

EXERCISE FOR YOU

How are you feeling right now after reading this lesson? It is okay if you do or don't know. If you need help with identifying your feeling(s), you can view a list of feelings on our blog at EngageCoachingGroup.com.

_____

_____

_____

_____

What is your experience with your feelings?

_____

_____

_____

_____

Do you tend to avoid or embrace your feelings?

_____

_____

_____

_____

How come?

_____

_____

_____

_____

EXERCISE FOR YOUR TEAM OR GROUP

What does it feel like to be a part of the team?

_____

_____

_____

_____

What are some specific reasons for the group members' answers to the question above? For instance, "How are you feeling right now after reading this lesson? What is your experience with your feelings? Do you tend to avoid or embrace your feelings?

_____

_____

_____

_____

Based on the reasons above, what is one thing the team should continue doing and one improvement it could make in this area?

_____

_____

_____

_____

NOTES

Lesson # 6

WHAT IS HOLDING YOU BACK?

For myself, it took me a number of years to realize the biggest thing holding me back from taking action in my life was the belief I needed to acquire something outside myself. I believed a new job, a new car, a new relationship, or more money would solve all my problems.

Below is a journal entry of mine from January 2000 on this topic.

JOURNAL ENTRY JANUARY 2000

Live every moment like it is your last. What has to happen to make this make sense in my life? Does something have to happen before I make the realization that life really is shorter than short? A near death experience, a natural disaster, a major accident that is survived, a loss of a loved one, losing your job, stubbing your toe or biting your lip? What about nothing? Can nothing happen to make me realize how short my life is? I'm so lucky to be given what I have, but yet I feel so selfish. I'm not satisfied with what I've got. I want more. I want it all or nothing. I just can't be satisfied with what I have now. I'm allowing my wants and desires to get the best of me. I thrive on impulse. Immediate recognition and gratification. Maybe it's this or maybe it's that. It's definitely something that I need to fix on my own. One cannot live on desires alone. Those desires will then be the norm and cause new desires to be created and sought after. Materials are loved by so many. Will they ever love us back? Will they ever not become old & used? Will they ever remain shiny & new? Will we stop caring for something that cannot love us back? We are now in love with our possessions. They don't think or talk back to us. Unless they are a person who has become someone's possession. People have become possessions too. We have all become only children.

EXERCISE FOR YOU

Spend some timing writing about what it is you truly want in life.

_____

_____

_____

_____

Is this in alignment with your intention you wrote earlier?

_____

_____

_____

_____

What barriers or struggles do you need to overcome to achieve what you want?

_____

_____

_____

_____

What are some realistic first steps to enable you to overcome the struggles?

_____

_____

_____

_____

EXERCISE FOR YOUR TEAM OR GROUP

Spend some timing writing about what it is your team or group truly wants.

_____

_____

_____

_____

Is this in alignment with your intention you wrote earlier?

_____

_____

_____

If not, how come?

_____

_____

_____

_____

What barriers or struggles do the team members need to overcome to achieve what all of you want?

_____

_____

_____

_____

What are some realistic first steps to enable you to overcome the struggles?

_____

_____

_____

_____

NOTES

Lesson # 7

YOUR THOUGHTS

What does that voice in your head want to say right now? Here is an example of me journaling about my thoughts.

JOURNAL ENTRY JULY 1, 2010

My Thoughts
It is time to get off my ass.
It is time to be a man.
It is time to go out of my comfort zone.
It time to stop planning & start asking.
It is time for me to enjoy and cherish every day.
It is time for me to plan meals and do it.
It is time for me to write more.
It is time for me to stop thinking I would fail at running a business.
It is time for me to start living my passion.
It is time for me to be romantic again.
It is time for me to stop living in the past & future.
It is time for now.
It is time for me to stop worrying about every freaking thing.
It is time for me to express my opinion.
It is time for me to have a backbone.
It is time for me to be the leader I was made to be.
It is time for me to be an optimist.
It is time to believe in the greater good.
It is time to be selfless.
It is time to truly care about others.

It is time to be compassionate.
It is time to stop looking at what I don't have.
It is time to enjoy the simple things in life.
It is time to live everyday like it is my last.
It is time to exercise more.
It is time to laugh more.
It is time to be a part of the community.
It is time to give back.
It is time to be me for me.
It is time to stop thinking somebody's always watching me.
It is time to be the father I aspire to be.
It is time to write self-help books to help others live their dreams.
It is time to be the teacher I have always wanted to be.
It is time to look beyond the politics.
It is time to see the big picture.
It is time to be healthy and energetic.
It is time to be full of love.
It is time for change like I have never faced before.
It is time to really live my life.
It is time to be present.
It is time to show the world that greed is not the answer.
It is time to not fall back into the rat race.
It is time to rise above the daily grind to see the ultimate destination.

EXERCISE FOR YOU

Spend some time letting the words come out to describe your thoughts, whatever they may be.

_____

_____

_____

_____

If you recall words from earlier in the day, feel free to write them as well.

_____

_____

_____

_____

Notice and write about how you felt as you wrote the words above.

_____

_____

_____

EXERCISE FOR YOUR TEAM OR GROUP

Have each member of the team write down their thoughts related to the team or group. These are immediate thoughts that come to mind or ones that could be ongoing through the day, week, or month.

_____

_____

_____

_____

As a group, have people share their thoughts with the rest of the group if people are open to it. Notice any similarities among members of the group.

_____

_____

_____

_____

As a group, spend some time discussing how sharing can help the group with its overall intention or goal.

_____

_____

_____

_____

Create some specific action steps to implement any new ideas or initiatives that have resulted from doing this exercise.

_____

_____

_____

_____

NOTES

Lesson # 8

YOUR STRUGGLE(S)

Are there struggles that continue to show up in your life? Here is a journal entry I wrote back in 2010 about a repeating pattern I noticed with my own struggles.

JOURNAL ENTRY DECEMBER 4, 2010

Patterns:

Questioned by people close to me—angry, irritated, tightness in chest, mind blocks

Argument—take it personally, want to be right, tightness in chest, mind black

Don't express my opinion unless I know someone else agrees with me

EXERCISE FOR YOU

What struggles continue to come up in your life? This could be related to communication, relationships, work, family, friends, etc.

_____

_____

_____

_____

When was the first time the struggle occurred in your life?

_____

_____

_____

_____

Who was there?

_____

_____

_____

_____

What do you remember about the experience?

_____

_____

_____

How did you feel?

_____

_____

_____

What similarities do you notice with your current struggle(s)?

_____

_____

_____

_____

What are some ideas about other ways you could approach your struggle(s)?

_____

_____

_____

_____

EXERCISE FOR YOUR TEAM OR GROUP

What struggles continue to come up with the team or group?

_____

_____

_____

_____

What patterns, if any, does the team or group notice with these struggles?

_____

_____

_____

_____

If people are open to it, have the group share their individual struggles and notice if there are any patterns or themes between the team struggle and the individual struggles. Write about them here.

_____

_____

_____

_____

With all this knowledge about the team or group struggle, what are some ideas about approaching it differently?

_____

_____

_____

_____

Lesson # 9

YOUR WORRIES

I have spent my life worrying a lot. It seems to be a common behaviour in my family. What do you worry about?

Here is an entry related to how I changed my focus on worrying about things.

JOURNAL ENTRY JUNE 22, 2003

I have said it many times. I am confident and I am my own person. I am not a follower. I am a leader. I find that I go through phases where I tend to follow others. I don't express my own opinion in fear of upsetting people. My opinion does count and I can tell people what I think. I don't have to worry about what they think of me. I can be confident that my opinion counts for something. I am quite focused right now, but I have to remember that I don't need to put others' thoughts in my head; just put my own thoughts there.

I am happy

I am confident

I have an exciting life

I am working toward my goals and dreams

Not every day is a party

Every day does count and I can do my best to make the most of it

I am patient, I am patient, I am patient

I value others' opinions

I don't always have to be right

I don't always have to be right.

EXERCISE FOR YOU

Do you worry a lot?

_____

_____

_____

_____

If so, what do you worry about?

_____

_____

_____

_____

If you don't worry about anything, write about how you are able to do this.

_____

_____

_____

_____

Do you doubt your abilities? If so, write about your doubts here.

_____

_____

_____

_____

If you have no doubts, write about how you are able to approach your life from this perspective.

_____

_____

_____

_____

If applicable, what are the benefits of having worries or doubts?

_____

_____

_____

_____

If applicable, how would you behave differently if you no longer had worries or doubts?

_____

_____

_____

_____

EXERCISE FOR YOUR TEAM OR GROUP

As a group, have an open discussion about the worries or doubts people are having. What are these worries?

_____

_____

_____

_____

How are these worries or doubts impacting the performance of the group?

_____

_____

_____

_____

How can the group use any worries or doubts to reinforce the overall goal or intention?

_____

_____

_____

_____

Lesson # 10

YOUR JUDGEMENT

I have spent a lot of my life being concerned about what others think about me. I would tend to misinterpret comments people said to me and assume it was an attack against me.

You can read some of my journal entries below related to this. I have recognized that the person who is actually judging me is myself.

JOURNAL ENTRY FEBRUARY 8, 2001

Nervous & I don't know why,
Embarrassed for things I've done,
Silent to not offend,
Worried about what others might say.

JOURNAL ENTRY FEBRUARY 19, 2001

Patient in how to react,
aware of the situation I'm in,
unsure how to proceed,
assuming others' thoughts,
watching every move,
analyzing every detail,
worried I am, why I don't know,
Alone in darkness and in light,
searching for whom, I don't know,
Focusing on each day to keep on track,
learning is what some may say,
hoping my decision will be in sight,
confident is how I need be

JOURNAL ENTRY SEPTEMBER 3, 2002

I am very concerned as to what others think of me.

I have difficulty making my own decisions without considering what others might think.

I still am concerned as to what people from my past think of me.

I put other people's thoughts in my head & make assumptions as to what they are thinking of me.

I worry a lot about little things over & over & over again.

I forget how lucky I am

I tend to sacrifice my time & well-being to satisfy others

I have trouble managing my time to do things I want

I have been lazy & give up easier when my confidence is low

I have trouble listening when my confidence is low

I gradually get stronger one day at a time.

JOURNAL ENTRY JANUARY 17, 2000

One must be brave,

One must be certain,

One must listen to thyself and not to others' negative thoughts,

Then one can be happy and feel.

EXERCISE FOR YOU

What is your experience with judgement? Write about this here.

_____

_____

_____

_____

Are these judgements actually true?

_____

_____

_____

_____

How would things be different for you if they were false?

_____

_____

_____

_____

EXERCISE FOR YOUR TEAM OR GROUP

Write about any judgements the team may be dealing with.

_____

_____

_____

_____

Is this team being judged a certain way in the organization?

_____

_____

_____

Are the team members judging the team as a whole in an unproductive way?

_____

_____

_____

_____

Are these judgements actually true?

_____

_____

_____

_____

How would things be different for the team if the judgements were false?

_____

_____

_____

_____

Lesson # 11

YOUR MISTAKES

What happens when you make a mistake? I have had my own challenges with putting added pressure on myself when I make a mistake.

JOURNAL ENTRY FEBRUARY 1, 1999

I have been doing a fair bit of writing in the last little bit. Maybe it's that time of the year. This past weekend has really hit hard. I did something quite stupid and was lucky the situation didn't get worse. I panicked like I have never done before. No control is no fun. I made a mistake and it hit me point blank. I kept saying over and over, I should have …. If only ….
I want to go back in time and correct my error. Of course, we all want to do this impossible task.

JOURNAL ENTRY JULY 11, 2000

I locked my keys in my car; I'm the CEO of the largest co. in the world.
I spilled hot coffee all over my new pants; I make 14 million dollars a movie.
I farted in public today; I'm the leader of this country.
My fly was down all day; I have my own talk show.
I forgot to call my mom on her birthday; I'm normal just like everybody else.
When I know I'm going to have to speak up in a group, my heart speeds up, I feel warm, I feel nervous, my mind loses focus on what I'm going to say, I keep repeating in my head what I'm going to say, I don't look at people I'm talking to, I blank them out until I'm done.
My mouth is moving, but I don't know what is coming out.

EXERCISE FOR YOU

What do you believe is going to happen if you make a mistake?

_____

_____

_____

_____

What actually happens to you when you make a mistake?

_____

_____

_____

_____

How do you handle it?

_____

_____

_____

_____

Do you accept it and learn from it?

_____

_____

_____

_____

Do you replay your mistake in your mind over and over?

_____

_____

_____

_____

Does it impact your self-confidence and/or your self-esteem?

_____

_____

_____

_____

What lessons have you learned from the mistakes you have made? Write about them here.

_____

_____

_____

_____

Lesson 11

EXERCISE FOR YOUR TEAM OR GROUP

What do you believe is going to happen if your team or group makes a mistake?

_____

_____

_____

_____

What actually happens when the team or group makes a mistake?

_____

_____

_____

_____

How does the team handle it?

_____

_____

_____

_____

71

Does the team accept it and learn from it?

_____

_____

_____

_____

Does the mistake impact the performance of the team?

_____

_____

_____

_____

What lessons has your team or group learned from the mistakes it has made? Write about them here.

_____

_____

_____

_____

Lesson # 12

YOUR LIFE STORIES

An exercise I found helpful to better understand myself was to write out stories from my life that taught me a life lesson about going within. For me, I started at kindergarten and wrote about things I remembered throughout my years in school. You may have a different reference point. The idea is to reflect back to the earliest events you remember in your life—good or bad—which were ultimately a potential lesson to guide you to learn more about who you are.

JOURNAL ENTRY SEPTEMBER 20, 2012

Here is something I wrote about some key moments in my life that impacted the beliefs I created about myself and the world. Seego was the dog we had when I was young.

giving Seego away

Grandpa passing

Getting lost in toy section of Sears

Moving from P.G. to W.L. in Kindergarten

Having really good friends and then they move away

almost failing grade 4

EXERCISE FOR YOU

Write about your life. Go back as far as you can remember. Write out stories when you were young, when you were in school, when you were a teenager. Write about the moments that have stayed with you all these years.

_____

_____

_____

_____

EXERCISE FOR YOUR TEAM OR GROUP

What are the stories about your company and your team?

_____

_____

_____

_____

NOTES

Lesson # 13

YOUR MENTAL HEALTH

I have struggled with depression for many years. I had symptoms of it in high school and I wasn't diagnosed until my mid- to late-twenties. Early on, I was afraid to tell others I struggled with it. I would only write about it and speak with my doctor and therapist about it.

JOURNAL ENTRY JANUARY 1999

Here are some journal entries I made over the years about my depression. You will notice text in italics for the journal entry from 2011. This italic text is the response I received from having a written conversation with my depression.

What does depression feel like? Everything seems very dark and dreamy through my eyes. I don't feel like the same person that I was when I was in Kamloops. Work is more of a routine than a challenge. I look forward to coming home and lying on the couch and doing nothing. What happened to my free caring mood? Is it the Big City Blues? I want to go somewhere hot and sunny all the time. I don't like clouds anymore. I feel less about myself. I feel like I have become more dependent on others to make me happy. I'm a good person and I don't have it even close to being bad. The only thing that sucks is everyone I know lives even farther away. I think I had it too good in Kamloops and now things seem dull in comparison.

JOURNAL ENTRY OCTOBER 2010

They say I am depressed,
here are the pills,
They make everything go calm & chill

I have been told that depression is anger turned in,
I just need to face it & say "not by the hair of my chinny, chin, chin."

The real cure is to breathe & feel it,
Go in & out,
Try my emotions & stop with the doubt.

There is so much light around me,
the darkness can be turned away,
This will ensure my thoughts don't continue to stay,

It is the self-talk which for me starts it all,
it becomes a strategic marketer like a fancy shopping mall.

The voice is trying to protect me, but
doesn't see I am safe & sound,
It assumed that I know nothing &
answers need to be found.

Answers to mistakes, to errors & silly things I say,
When all it needs to do is focus on the moment of today.

JOURNAL ENTRY DECEMBER 31, 2011

Hello, depression. There is about 30 minutes left in 2011 and I wanted to thank you.
You have taught me so much in 2011 and previous years. You have shown me how I don't
want to live my life. you have shown me how easy it can be to lose what I cherish. You have
shown me how it feels to do work solely for the money. you have shown me what it is like
to not have a social life or romantic life. you have allowed me to experience anxiety and
nervousness. you have brought thoughts into my mind that I didn't think existed. you have
shown me what it is like to feel numb, emotionless and heartless. it has made me realize that
this is not how I want to feel. I am viewing it as an opportunity to begin living for the moment
with my heart in full force. because of this I will no longer require your services at this time. I
desire to be full of light and warmth, peace and joy. I now know I am never alone and can live

anxiety free. thank you for the time you have spent showing me this.

What are your thoughts about this?

I am not completely surprised, however I do feel that we have become so close over the years. It feels like you want to be rid of me and never want to hear from me. I thought we would spend more time together.

It sounds like you really care about me. would you want to see me live the best possible life?

Yes, of course, as down as you have been I never wanted to hurt you and see you harmed. I know deep down this day would come. I didn't think it would be this soon. I will do as you wish. I will leave your aura, your body, your space and allow you to receive light and joy. you will be able to focus better, your memory will noticeably improve. you will find no need for medication. this is my gift to you for 2012 and beyond.

Thank you, depression. I appreciate everything you have done for me. Take care and bring more awakenings to others you meet.

EXERCISE FOR YOU

Have you or friends or family experienced mental illness?

_____

_____

_____

_____

Write about your experience with your own mental health.

_____

_____

_____

How does this experience impact how you interact with your friends, family, work, and so on?

_____

_____

_____

EXERCISE FOR YOUR TEAM OR GROUP

The topic of "stress" can be an easy conversation starter, as most people can talk about their experience with stress. What is your team or group's experience with stress and mental health?

_____

_____

_____

_____

What steps can this group take to help strengthen the mental state of the group on a regular basis?

_____

_____

_____

_____

NOTES

Lesson # 14

RELEASE YOUR NEGATIVE THOUGHTS

I had moments when I needed to get negative thought out of my head. I would use my journal as a way to do this. Below is something I wrote in March 2000 about how I was feeling at the time.

JOURNAL ENTRY MARCH 19, 2000

I'm feeling isolated. I don't know if that's the word, but I don't feel like talking to anybody. It's like someone could say whatever they wanted to me & I would just sit there not replying. Little things have been frustrating me. It's like I just want to hide in my room for a while. My self-esteem has depleted & I don't know why. This seems to happen every few months.

Nothing in my head,

Nothing out of my mouth,

All is hiding, nowhere to be found,

I feel better alone,

With no one around,

It makes things easier,

I'm in control of the nothing in my head,

Until I have to go,

Maybe I'll just stay,

Find something new,

That's when I feel better,

Until it becomes new no more,

I desire new,

One day I sense it's new no more,

It's now old & used,

It doesn't look or feel the same as when I first got it,

I've become used to it,

It no longer excites me,
I cause this to happen,
I only savour the beginning & don't,
Look down the road,
If it doesn't work by now,
Don't forget that no matter what,
You learn something new every day.

EXERCISE FOR YOU

There are many ways you can release negativity from your mind. Try writing about your negative thoughts or try one of the ways I list below.

1. Use journaling to write out everything that bothers you. You can then read it over and see if it really is impacting you that much.

2. Record yourself saying all the negative things on your mind then notice how you feel afterwards. Delete the recording if you don't feel comfortable keeping it.

3. Record a video of yourself expressing your thoughts. You could watch it and see yourself in a different light. Just by seeing yourself in that state of mind may trigger you to view things differently. Delete the recording if you don't feel comfortable keeping it.

4. Talk with someone about the problems you are facing, whether it be a friend, family member, college, doctor, counsellor, life coach, or someone else.

_____

_____

_____

_____

Review what you did and reflect on what you thought about it and what these thoughts are giving you. What is their purpose?

_____

_____

_____

_____

How can you look at these thoughts differently?

_____

_____

_____

_____

Lesson 14

EXERCISE FOR YOUR TEAM OR GROUP

As a group, if people are open to it, your team can spend some time sharing any negative thoughts they are having, which could be impacting their ability to be fully engaged in their work. Write about these here.

_____

_____

_____

_____

It is important to provide a safe environment for people to share with the group. The intention of sharing should be focused on allowing people to share without judgement. Based on what the team has shared, how can the team use this learning as a way to move forward to keep in alignment with the team's overall goal or intention?

_____

_____

_____

_____

NOTES

Lesson # 15

YOUR FEARS

I have had moments in my life when fear has set in and the thoughts in my head have taken over. Below are some examples of my journal entries related to this.

JOURNAL ENTRY FROM 2005

Once something gets difficult or challenging—job, relationships, commitments—I get overwhelmed and have a hard time focusing. I focus on the negative. I become quiet and have trouble responding to people when they ask my opinion. I don't spend time properly, day to day stuff like laundry, dishes, cleaning become overwhelming in addition to my life goals.

Things Got Difficult so I withdrew:

High School Basketball

University

Relationships

Presentations at school

Sales positions for work

JOURNAL ENTRY FROM 2005

I put others in my head,

I mumble more, talk faster,

I would rather give up than fix things,

I am quiet and everyone thinks something is wrong with me,

I fear losing my job,

Everyone is looking at me funny and thinking I am acting weird,

Everyone knows I could lose my job,

I feel like a fly on the wall and I'm watching myself from a distance,
I can't remember anything,
I can't afford to do anything

JOURNAL ENTRY FEBRUARY 10, 2013

Fear is what drives your ego. Your ego is afraid that if you start focusing on good, it will be out of a job.

The real job of the ego is protecting you from death. The ego's job has been glorified to the point where it is completely over-functioning. It is taking on too much. It should focus on what it was intended for, survival.

Do you need the latest tech gadget to survive? Your ego may think so. Do you need food, water, sleep & exercise to survive? Yes & your ego has construed what that looks like. Plus it gets distracted by all the media telling it to convince you to buy junk food over healthy food, sit on the couch versus exercise.

EXERCISE FOR YOU

Spend some time writing about times when fear sets in for you. What goes through your mind during these times?

_____

_____

_____

_____

Perhaps, there are certain behaviours that occur when fear is running things. Is this so for you?

_____

_____

_____

_____

A powerful exercise is to write about what you believe will happen if your worst fears occur. What might happen?

_____

_____

_____

_____

What is the possibility for the end result to actually happening?

_____

_____

_____

_____

What else could actually be happening that is causing the fear in the first place?

_____

_____

_____

_____

EXERCISE FOR YOUR TEAM OR GROUP

If the group has fears related to work, the group members may want to spend some time sharing their answers to the previous exercise.

_____

_____

_____

_____

What actions can your team take to help each other remember what is actually happening when fears arise?

_____

_____

_____

_____

NOTES

Lesson # 16

YOUR SELF-WORTH

The fear mentioned in the last exercise can impact how we feel and ultimately how we value our self. Here are two journal entries from different times in my life for you to see how my approach to my situation shifted.

JOURNAL ENTRY OCTOBER 3, 2002

I have come to the conclusion that I have self-confidence issues, low self-esteem and a lack assertiveness at times. A lot of it depends on what I think someone thinks of me or how they see me. I think the periods I have when I feel really confident are when I have had several occurrences of thinking people are thinking highly of me. I get really embarrassed when I need to give my opinion or speak. My job is cool and all, but I feel that I am holding back because of a fear of rejection. It is the same cycle over and over again.

Plus, I am not busy and on the go, so I have time to ponder. My pondering tends to focus on my negative attributes then the positive at times. I am a positive person, but I really put a lot of pressure on little things that don't mean too much in the grand scheme of things. I feel lost and don't really know my purpose. My goals include paying off my debt, travelling, buying property, doing fun things, being happy, travelling some more, eventually get married and kids and all that. boring? I think yup. Where is my creativity and my drive? I seem to forget about my needs and keep trying to please others.

JOURNAL ENTRY MARCH 10, 2012

I learned today that my ego does things to show me what I need to hear.
I learned that I can realize the truth of the benefits of my feelings. There is fear within me that is not required right now. It can be better used when real danger is here.
I am a good father.

95

I am lovable.

I matter.

Thank you, God, for your guidance today.

Bless you with all my love.

EXERCISE FOR YOU

What specifically do you value about yourself?

_____

_____

_____

_____

How much do you value yourself? Spend some time writing your answers.

_____

_____

_____

If you are feeling low or down, are there any ways you can view things differently?

_____

_____

_____

_____

EXERCISE FOR YOUR TEAM OR GROUP

What do members value about being part of your team or group?

_____

_____

_____

_____

What can each member do collectively to remember this regularly?

_____

_____

_____

_____

Lesson # 17

CLEAR YOUR MIND

An exercise I find very helpful at times is to write out everything that is going on in my head. I have provided an example of a journal entry below.

JOURNAL ENTRY JULY 20, 2011

So much in my head.

I am taking no action to improve my situation.

I am a follower and scared to take a stand or contribute.

I show no emotion, excitement, joy.

I put up a wall to protect myself from pain, a fear of losing.

I am constantly focused on how I can make more money, how to find time to exercise and do fun things.

I don't feel present.

I continue to seek help from outside.

I continue to explore new careers or business opportunities.

I have trouble focusing and end up not getting a lot done.

I need your help, guidance & support to get through this.

EXERCISE FOR YOU

Write out whatever is going on in your head. Good, bad, ugly. Write it out and notice what happens.

_____

_____

_____

_____

A powerful question to ask yourself after you do this is, What are you making it mean about yourself?

_____

_____

_____

_____

Is that actually true?

_____

_____

_____

_____

What is the truth about yourself, considered from a place of compassion and understanding?

_____

_____

_____

_____

EXERCISE FOR YOUR TEAM OR GROUP

As a team or group, you could spend some time allowing people to share their thoughts about the team.

_____

_____

_____

_____

How can you use this information to make improvements to the productivity of your team?

_____

_____

_____

_____

Lesson # 18

YOUR PRESENT STATE

I have struggled for a long time and still do with remaining present. I learned at a young age to go into the past and future regularly. Here is a journal entry related to this.

JOURNAL ENTRY MID-1990S

Do we tend to say and believe we are happy, when in fact we are absolutely miserable? What would make us want to be such a thing? I'm not saying I'm miserable, but when you look toward the future & don't know what to see, it's really scary. I'm really feeling afraid of the future. Why do I feel this way? Not knowing should make things even more exciting. I think I just want to know everything will be alright and I figure everything out in one day. I think worrying about it is not the answer. Life is way too short to spend it worrying. I enjoy each day the best I can and live for the now as much as I can. Like that is easy to do!

EXERCISE FOR YOU

Spend some time for the next few days becoming aware of yourself and the things around you. Your thoughts, your breathing, your feelings, the things you look at, the things you hear, the wind, the smells, and the tastes. Become an observer of your life. You can journal about this so you can look back and observe any patterns and themes.

_____

_____

_____

_____

EXERCISE FOR YOUR TEAM OR GROUP

Share the personal exercise above with your team so everyone can work on it individually. Then, the team can spend time having people share what they wrote about their experience.

_____

_____

_____

_____

NOTES

Lesson # 19

YOUR COMMUNICATION

Over the years, one thing I finally recognized was there was a specific way I was communicating with myself. I realized I had been essentially bullying myself based on the words, negativity, and tone I used.

Here are some journal entries I wrote that are related to my communication with myself.

JOURNAL ENTRY NOVEMBER 23, 2011

I am a fake. I am a phony. My ego has run my life for as long as I can remember. I am virtually sleepwalking through the days. I want what Eckhart Tolle & Neale Donald Walsch have. I want the understanding & the being.

JOURNAL ENTRY NOVEMBER 2011

Me right now. I am a people pleaser. A coward. boring. I worry a lot. I am no fun. I have no interests. I am not exciting to be around. I am in the wrong profession. I love being a Dad. I have no opinion. I follow versus lead. I don't have friends. I am invisible. I am not memorable. I am quiet. I am lost. I worry about what others think. I need help. I have so much. I have a lovely family.

EXERCISE FOR YOU

How do you communicate with yourself? List the words you use. Is the tone, critical, inspiring, positive, loving?

Spend throughout the day noticing how you are communicating with yourself.

Is this method of communicating moving you closer to or further away from your goal?

_____

_____

_____

_____

How come?

_____

_____

_____

_____

What is one thing you would change to improve the way you communicate with yourself?

_____

_____

_____

_____

EXERCISE FOR YOUR TEAM OR GROUP

How does your team or group communicate with the other members of the team? List the words people use. Is the tone, critical, inspiring, positive, loving?

_____

_____

_____

_____

Is this method of communicating moving the team closer to or further away from its goal?

_____

_____

_____

_____

How come?

_____

_____

_____

_____

What is one thing your team would change to improve the way you communicate with each other?

_____

_____

_____

_____

NOTES

Lesson # 20

WHEN YOU FEEL LIKE YOU

Over the years, I have had a number of times in my life when all the worries, doubts, judgements and so on seemed to disappear. Everything seemed clearer. As I get older, I am having these moments more often. I am overwhelmed with gratitude, happiness, and peace with my life.

Here is a journal entry from 2007 when I felt like myself.

JOURNAL ENTRY MAY 25, 2007

I feel like the fog has left,
I feel energized again,
I feel excited,
I feel like I have a purpose,
I feel confident,
I feel focused,
I feel like laughing more,
I feel like having fun,
I feel like being silly,
I feel like a meaningful person,
I feel loved,
I feel like me.

EXERCISE FOR YOU

Write about the times in your life when you truly and absolutely feel like yourself. Close your eyes and go to those times. What do you see?

_____

_____

_____

_____

What do you hear?

_____

_____

_____

_____

What do you feel?

_____

_____

_____

_____

What does your heart say to you during those moments?

_____

_____

_____

_____

How can you access the sights, sounds, and feelings related to this feeling?

_____

_____

_____

_____

How can you like your true self on a regular basis?

_____

_____

_____

_____

EXERCISE FOR YOUR TEAM OR GROUP

Write about times when your team has performed in an efficient, productive, collaborative, understanding, and amazing way.

_____

_____

_____

_____

If this is a new team, imagine what it would be like if your team were performing at its highest potential.

_____

_____

_____

_____

What might the team see?

_____

_____

_____

_____

What might the team hear?

_____

_____

_____

_____

What might the team feel?

_____

_____

_____

_____

What does the heart of the team say to itself during those moments?

_____

_____

_____

_____

How can the team access the sights, sounds, and feelings related to feeling like a high productive team on a regular basis?

_____

_____

_____

_____

Lesson # 21

REVIEW LESSONS 1 TO 20

Now is an opportunity to review the work you have done so far. You have done some great work . Review all of the journal entries you have made from this section of the workbook and then work through the questions below.

EXERCISE FOR YOU

What did you learn about yourself?

_____

_____

_____

_____

What patterns have you noticed about yourself?

_____

_____

_____

_____

What exercises did you find the most helpful for you?

_____

_____

_____

_____

How come?

_____

_____

_____

_____

What are three things you can do to ensure you are fully engaged in reaching your goal or intention?

_____

_____

_____

_____

EXERCISE FOR YOUR TEAM OR GROUP

Individuals can share their answers to their own questions if they are open to it. What has the group learned collectively from the past twenty-one lessons?

_____

_____

_____

_____

What stands out as high-impact learnings for the group?

_____

_____

_____

_____

Lesson 21

What three things can the group do to ensure it is collectively and fully engaged in its goal or intention?

_____

_____

_____

_____

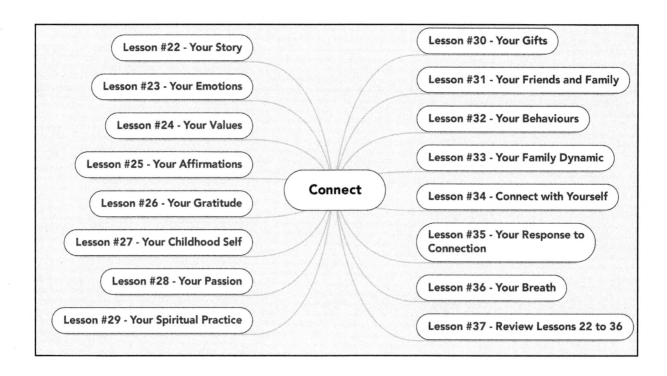

Part 2
CONNECT

"Before you can ever inspire, motivate, or influence, you must connect first." Greg Smith

The definition of "to connect" is "to bring together or into contact so that either a real or a notional link is established."

Now that you have completed the initial twenty-two lessons focused on engaging, you will now work through the lessons focused on connecting.

The intention of these exercises is to guide you toward an improved connection with yourself, your team, and others in your life. You will be given the opportunity to bring additional connection to areas such as your story, your emotions, and your values.

As with the last section, I invite you to be open to the lessons. Be sure to spend quality time on them by getting to know yourself and your team better.

It is also helpful to keep your intention in mind from lesson two. This intention is the destination of where you are headed and what is truly important to you. It is ultimately why you are doing these exercises.

Lesson # 22

YOUR STORY

I know for myself, I have spent a lot of my life attached to my story. I tended to blame others and myself for the state of my situation.

I grew up in a small town. I was a shy, quiet, awkward boy. I played basketball and volleyball in high school. I was a B-average student. I watch movies, played video games. I didn't have girlfriends and I didn't go to a lot of the parties. I played a variety of sports with my friends. I felt different. I would have times in high school when I felt good about myself and then I would go through weeks when I felt as small as a pebble. As I grew older, I continued to feel "less than" and I tried to find ways to feel more confident and included in groups.

Over time, I learned so much about myself. I now recognize my past prepared me for where I am now. I wouldn't have been able to write this workbook without going through all the experiences I have had. I see my story differently. I am grateful for where I have come from. I have learned so much along the way.

EXERCISE FOR YOU

Write your life story. Choose one story to start with. You can start from the first memory you have or a major life event when you were young.

_____

_____

_____

_____

What do you connect most with related to your life story?

_____

_____

_____

_____

How come you connect most with this?

_____

_____

_____

_____

Do you find yourself regretting parts of your life?

_____

_____

_____

_____

Do you find yourself wishing things were better?

_____

_____

_____

_____

What theme comes to mind when you reflect on your life story?

_____

_____

_____

_____

What do you want most to be remembered for?

_____

_____

_____

_____

EXERCISE FOR YOUR TEAM OR GROUP

If people are open to it, team members can share their answers about themselves. This can be a great way for people to get to know each other better. What is the story or stories you tell about this team?

_____

_____

_____

_____

What stories, if any, take the group away from its goal?

_____

_____

_____

_____

What stories, if any, move the group toward its goal?

_____

_____

_____

_____

What aspects of the team story do you want to keep and use to allow the team to grow?

_____

_____

_____

_____

Lesson # 23

YOUR EMOTIONS

I spent a lot of my life misunderstanding my emotions and literally being disconnected from them. One emotion I struggled a lot with was anger. I tended to hold on to my anger. A number of years ago, a therapist shared with me that anger turned inward is depression.

An extra note about anger. Anger is a surface emotion. The true emotion is hidden underneath it. What I learned about anger is it is important to release it in a safe way. Writing about it can be one way to do this. Then you want to connect to how you are feeling underneath the anger. You can also explore when you first experienced the feeling underneath the anger.

For me, when I released the anger, I experienced tremendous sadness. Sadness that I had been holding on to for many, many years. I had been avoiding feeling it for so long. When I let the sadness happen, I felt so much weight being lifted.

It is okay to feel your emotions. Use this lesson to give yourself permission to allow them to come forward and notice what happens. You can write more about your experience below.

JOURNAL ENTRY MID-1990S

Hello, my name is Aaron,

Anger is something I don't feel too regularly,

It doesn't seem to be in my nature,

For some reason tonight is my night to let loose,

The reason is obvious to me, but it is like a disease,

A disease I can't cure and may not ever cure,

Who knows why, who knows what?

I've never been so pissed off in my life,

Is it the alcohol? Maybe?

Can I spell beer, maybe not!

The disease is taking me over and I don't know what to do,

135

It is everywhere, I can't stop it,
I can't cure it at the moment,
Once again all I can do is ignore it and hope, just f&*in hope
it will go away. (I'm not religious, but I'll pray anyway)
I need a CURE!!!

JOURNAL ENTRY FEBRUARY 20, 2000

I felt anger like I haven't in a long time. Triggered by a little bull shit that I couldn't handle. I feel frustrated, mad, tense, all at the same time. I just want to release it by punching or squeezing something.

Mondays I always feel the same. I'm tired & don't want anything or anyone to bother me. My eyes feel heavy & my brain won't focus on anything for too long. I feel like I'm up way earlier than I should be.

JOURNAL ENTRY MAY 3, 2012

So, what am I so sad & angry about? Why has it built up in me for so long? What is the worst case scenario if I continue avoiding these feelings? Career? Sickness? Unfulfilled life? Disconnected relationships with others? Not living my passion? More pain? More fear? Less Peace? It seems like there is a lot of downside to remain as is. So what good will come of feeling this sadness/angry etc. and getting to the forefront of my awareness. Less weight? Less burden? more love, joy & peace? Close to my family? Improved communication? A life of passion? Being real? Being authentic? Loving me? Writing books to share my learnings? Financial freedom? Spiritual awareness? A greater community of loving people? So a long list of real & true benefits to going on this straight on. Look forward to it. I can do this. I can feel it. I am ready. God, show me the way inward to peace, joy & love. I want in!

So what does this sadness & anger feel like? Where do I feel it? It is primarily in my stomach. Typically feelings of tightness, nervousness, worry in the left side of my stomach. I also had tightness in my chest which goes away when the area in my stomach is activated. It feels at times like a baseball inside me. Very solid with some motion. It impacts my decisions. It tends to have diarrhea at times & I am constipated. Deep breathing seems to help the best to relieve the tension as well as cardio exercise. The mass if you will seems to believe it is needed to protect me. I had various bits of bad news in my past. Grandpa dying and our dog being given away. My stomach pain believes it is better to worry about possible scenarios to be prepared for bad things that happen.

EXERCISE FOR YOU

Use this time to write about your relationship with your emotions. Which emotions do you access with ease?

_____

_____

_____

_____

Which emotions do you tend to avoid?

_____

_____

_____

_____

How connected do you feel to your emotions?

_____

_____

_____

_____

How do your emotions impact your life?

_____

_____

_____

What can you do to connect to your emotions in a way that helps you continue to move toward your intention?

_____

_____

_____

_____

EXERCISE FOR YOUR TEAM OR GROUP

If the team is open to it, you can spend time having team members share their answers to the above questions. The goal here is to bring the team closer together by allowing people to share their experience with their emotions. How does this team or group respond when emotions are being expressed?

_____

_____

_____

_____

Is it okay to express emotions in this team or group?

_____

_____

_____

_____

If no, how come?

_____

_____

_____

_____

If yes, how come?

_____

_____

_____

_____

How can the open expression of emotions help the group move closer to its goal or intention?

_____

_____

_____

_____

Lesson # 24

YOUR VALUES

What values do you live by? In 2012, 2013, and the years following, I did a lot of work on my values. I was able to define them better. I was able to determine which ones worked for me and which ones I didn't want to follow any longer.

JOURNAL ENTRY SEPTEMBER 8, 2012

What do I truly value? My health, my family, living my purpose, friendships, trust, and honesty are the key things I value.

JOURNAL ENTRY JULY 7, 2013

Values of a Man

Trusting

Generous

Gentle

Organized

Compassionate

Visionary

Passionate

Active father

Creative

Happy

Loving

Protective

Supportive

Loyal

Confident

Flexible

Open

Independent

EXERCISE FOR YOU

What do you truly value? Values are within your core and non-negotiable.

_____

_____

_____

_____

What values come to mind that are true to you? Write them out. If needed, you can review a list of values at www.EngageCoachingGroup.com. Review the list of values and write down the ones that you gravitate to. Make a short list of three to six and spend some time living with these values. Review them daily. You can journal about your experience when it comes to living your values.

_____

_____

_____

_____

EXERCISE FOR YOUR TEAM OR GROUP

If people are open to it, they can share with everyone their own individual values.

_____

_____

_____

_____

What values are important to the team?

_____

_____

_____

_____

NOTES

Lesson # 25

YOUR AFFIRMATIONS

What you say to yourself daily can have a huge impact on how you feel and ultimately how you view the world around you. Here are some of my journal entries in which I was writing out some affirmations for myself.

JOURNAL ENTRY MARCH 19, 2012

I am valuable—I matter

I am valuable—I matter

I am valuable—I matter

I am valuable—I matter

I am valuable—I matter

I am valuable—I matter

I am valuable—I matter

I am valuable—I matter

I am valuable—I matter

Journal Entry January 11, 2013

I am important.

I am scared.

I am worth it.

I have a voice.

I matter.

I can be me.

I can be myself.

I can be authentic.

I can be vulnerable.

I am free.

I have a say in this.
I am important.
I am worthy.
I will use my voice
I will be curious.
I will listen.
I will use my voice.
I am full of love.
I am full of light.

EXERCISE FOR YOU

What messages do you want to say to yourself regularly? Spend the next seven days writing about them here. Start now.

_____

_____

_____

_____

What messages do you want to stop saying to yourself?

_____

_____

_____

What existing or new affirmations do you want to continue saying to yourself?

_____

_____

_____

EXERCISE FOR YOUR TEAM OR GROUP

The group can share with each other the individual messages they want to continue saying to themselves regularly.

_____

_____

_____

_____

Are there any affirmations the group would find helpful?

_____

_____

_____

_____

Could those affirmations be posted up in the office or said together to help reinforce the group goal or intention?

_____

_____

_____

Lesson # 26

YOUR GRATITUDE

A powerful exercise for helping stay connected with yourself is practising gratitude. Here is a collection of journal entries from 2008 when I wrote regularly about what I was grateful for.

JOURNAL ENTRY JANUARY 6, 2008

I am grateful for the achievements I have made.

I am grateful for the knowledge I have.

I am grateful for the opportunities available to me and my family.

I am grateful I have a pen to be able to write what I am grateful for.

JOURNAL ENTRY JANUARY 9, 2008

I am grateful for my health.

I am grateful for my confidence today.

I am grateful that I could pay to fill up the car with gas.

JOURNAL ENTRY JANUARY 10, 2008

I am grateful for the friends in my life.

JOURNAL ENTRY JANUARY 13, 2008

I am grateful for my life. I have so much to not complain about. I am happier than I think.

JOURNAL ENTRY JANUARY 16, 2008

I am grateful that I can add value to other people's lives.

JOURNAL ENTRY JANUARY 30, 2008

I am grateful to have a secure warm place to live.

JOURNAL ENTRY JANUARY 31, 2008

I am grateful for the free Aikido Gi I received today.
I am grateful for the great client meeting I had today.
I am grateful for the food I had today.
I am grateful for my health.
I am grateful for those that love me.

JOURNAL ENTRY FEBRUARY 1, 2008

I am grateful for the positive people in my life.

EXERCISE FOR YOU

What things are you grateful for? Spend some time journaling what they are. This can be an exercise you do regularly such as daily or weekly. It can help reinforce what is truly important in your life regardless of any struggles that are occurring.

_____

_____

_____

_____

EXERCISE FOR YOUR TEAM OR GROUP

You can spend some time having the team share their individual answers.

_____

_____

_____

_____

What is the group collectively grateful for?

_____

_____

_____

_____

Lesson # 27

YOUR CHILDHOOD SELF

I learned this technique at a workshop I took in February 2012 through Clearmind International. Writing with your non-dominant hand can help you connect within yourself. You can find answers and ultimately healing when you spend some time connecting with the child within you. Below are some examples of connecting with the child inside of me. I wrote them all with my left hand.

JOURNAL ENTRY MARCH 15, 2012

Hello from the basement
I wanted to check in.
How are you feeling? I am here.
I am awake. I am lonely.
I don't know how to connect better with you. I find the door here closed.
Come visit me. Hold me. Love me.

JOURNAL ENTRY JUNE 13, 2012

Hello from the basement.
I am here. Where r you?
I want to talk to you.
I want to know you.
You are special to me.
I miss you.
You seem distant again.
Are you ok?
I feel alone again.
I miss you.

JOURNAL ENTRY NOVEMBER 18, 2012

Hello from the basement. The lights haven't been working for quite some time.
In Feb, you came to talk to me & I thought we would see more of each other. I miss you.
You seem lonely yourself. You seem to be needing something or wanting something. You
may be looking in the wrong place. I can help you. You can help me. We can heal together.
I want to get to know you & allow you to get to know me. I am the little boy who went to
perform & write & play. I want to show you how to do it. You are going to make such a major
positive impact on the love of people in the world. You will be doing this before you know how.
I am so full of pain. Please hold me. Please talk to me. Please love me. I am so alone in the
basement. I really would like to love life or the next love where I can see the light. The light
feels so warm. It feels like love. Do you feel love? It is amazing. You are full of so much love.
You just need to be open be open to feeling it, be open to seeing it. be open to expressing
it. be open, Aaron. be open with love & the world. and your full life. Your love is a gift, a gift
unique to you. You can share it immediately if you are open to it. Don't be afraid. Ask for help
if you need it. just ask for help.
love you, from the basement.

EXERCISE FOR YOU

Before you begin, find a quiet place, take some deep calming breaths, then put your pen in your non-dominant hand. Write to yourself as a child. What do you want to tell your childhood self?

_____

_____

_____

_____

What do you want to share with your childhood self?

_____

_____

_____

_____

Moving forward, what would you like your relationship with your childhood self to be?

_____

_____

_____

_____

What have your learned from this exercise?

_____

_____

_____

_____

EXERCISE FOR YOUR TEAM OR GROUP

If the team or group is open to it, each individual can share what they wrote to their childhood self.

_____

_____

_____

_____

What things does the group collectively learn from this exercise and how can it help improve how the group works together?

_____

_____

_____

_____

NOTES

Lesson # 28

YOUR PASSION

I believe we each have a fiery passion inside of us to share with the world. I have spent a number of years trying to understand mine and to fully connect to it. Journal entries like the ones below helped me with connecting to my passion.

JOURNAL ENTRY JANUARY 18, 2002

Are we all searching for the wrong thing?
Are we all searching in the wrong place?
Do we know what we are searching for?
How long will our search take?
Are we all searching with the right tools?
Are we all searching with the wrong tools?
When did we start searching?
How did we decide to start searching?
Or is there no searching going on?

JOURNAL ENTRY MARCH 27, 2009

I focused, I believed, I acted.
I knew what I wanted and I went for it,
I can teach this to others,
I can allow others to see what they want and go for it,
I can write books on things that most people desire in life and not material things.

EXERCISE FOR YOU

What would you do every day for the rest of your life if it could be anything?

_____

_____

_____

_____

How does this make a positive impact on your family, community, country, and the world?

_____

_____

_____

_____

If you have trouble defining this, it is okay. It can take time to see exactly what you want to do. You can make a list of times in your life when you felt completely fulfilled and knew you were contributing to others in a positive way.

_____

_____

_____

_____

EXERCISE FOR YOUR TEAM OR GROUP

The team can have everyone share their answers from the individual exercise for this lesson if people are open to it.

_____

_____

_____

_____

What is the group as a whole passionate about?

_____

_____

_____

How can the team access this passion on a regular basis?

_____

_____

_____

Lesson # 29

YOUR SPIRITUAL PRACTICE

I grew up going to Sunday School at an Anglican church. I primarily went because it meant every Sunday I got to hang out with my best friend. As I grew older, I stopped going to Sunday School and I didn't follow any religion. Over the years, I learned a variety of lessons from a spiritual perspective. I always tended to have more questions and concerns. It took me until my late thirties to really start exploring my spiritual beliefs and defining them for myself.

JOURNAL ENTRY APRIL 16, 2009

Here is a journal entry from 2009 when I really began believing in something bigger than myself.

I am excited about the future.
My mind is opening to the potential I can achieve.
I help people see past their challenges.
I help people see through their challenges.
I help people believe they can.
I help people achieve peace.
God wants me to show others the truth.
God wants me to lead others to peace.
How do I do this?
I am lying here on our couch feeling a bit overwhelmed. I know some of what I want or what my purpose is yet I am challenged with taking all the resources to clearly define it.
Mission/Purpose: God wants me to lead others to peace through their passion.

JOURNAL ENTRY DECEMBER 29, 2013, 10:25 P.M.

In 2013, I was introduced to *A Course in Miracles* and in 2014 I found myself writing directly to

God. For me, "God" represents something bigger than myself—the universe, the creator, mother nature. I have found a lot of benefits in recognizing there is a spiritual aspect to my life.

From A Course in Miracles , "You see what you believe is there and you believe it there because you want it there" (Chapter 25).

"'You will rejoice at what you see because you see it to rejoice'" (Chapter 25).

"Everything that comes from love is a miracle" (Chapter 1).

"Prayer is the medium of miracles. Prayer is the natural communication of the created with the creator" (Chapter 1).

JOURNAL ENTRY JUNE 13, 2014

Thank you, God. I appreciate you giving me so much right now. Patience is definitely something I will focus on. Time will tell.

EXERCISE FOR YOU

What do you want to journal about regarding spirituality? Perhaps your life experience with spirituality?

_____

_____

_____

_____

Do you have any questions about your spirituality?

_____

_____

_____

_____

Any struggles regarding it? Anything goes. You can journal it.

_____

_____

_____

_____

EXERCISE FOR YOUR TEAM OR GROUP

This may or may not be something the group is open to sharing at this point. If people are open to it, they can share their answers to the above questions.

In what ways could spirituality help this team or group continue to move towards its goal or intention?

Are there ways the team or group would like to learn more about spirituality?

_____

_____

_____

_____

Are there things about spirituality that the team or group would like to consider practising in some way?

_____

_____

_____

_____

Lesson # 30

YOUR GIFTS

In lesson 12, you were asked to write about stories in your life—those moments which have stayed with you all these years. These moments can provide clues about the gifts you have to offer to the world.

When I was a child, I listened really well. I also tended to sit back and observe before taking action. I was very conscious of the impact a decision could have on others. I would be quiet when I was unsure of what to do. I could look at these skills as negative or as positive. My ability to listen, observe, show empathy, and take time to make decisions are all tremendous skills for me to use as a coach and counsellor.

EXERCISE FOR YOU

Review your life stories from week thirteen. When you read them reflect on what you learned and what specific skills you used at those times in your life. For example, when I was younger there were several times I remember getting lost at the mall or at a large event. I became very resourceful as a child to find ways to find my parents. What are your reflections?

_____

_____

_____

_____

What skills did you have access to during these times of your life? These skills make you unique. These are your gifts.

_____

_____

_____

_____

EXERCISE FOR YOUR TEAM OR GROUP

You can have your team spend some time sharing their individual gifts. What did they say?

_____

_____

_____

_____

As a group you can discuss what people learned about this exercise.

_____

_____

_____

_____

How can the awareness of everyone's gifts help bring the team closer together to reach the team's goal or intention?

_____

_____

_____

_____

What three actions steps can the team take to take advantage of the gifts of the members that can help the team or group succeed?

_____

_____

_____

_____

Lesson # 31

YOUR FRIENDS AND FAMILY

I had times when I was depressed when it felt best to be on my own. I couldn't look people in the eye due to my fear of them seeing what was really going on for me. What I have experienced is when I stayed connected with people in my life as best I could, it helped me move through my depressed state. I didn't necessarily share everything that was going on for me. I made sure even when I was struggling to be around friends and family who I know supported me no matter what. Their presence gave me strength.

JOURNAL ENTRY DECEMBER 18, 2007

I am grateful for life's reminders of what is important. I am seeing that friends and family are what is most important. Europeans have already figured that out. It is obvious to see but not so obvious to live & breathe it.

JOURNAL ENTRY DECEMBER 21, 2007

I am grateful for the holiday season and how it brings families together to experience what this time of year and life for that matter is all about.

JOURNAL ENTRY DECEMBER 22, 2007

I am grateful for the time that is spent talking about family adventures—past & present.
I am grateful that I have so many good memories of my past. I pray that others can have the same types of fun.

EXERCISE FOR YOU

Write out your ideas for how you can connect with friends and family.

_____

_____

_____

_____

What step can you take today to make that connection happen in the next few days?

_____

_____

_____

_____

EXERCISE FOR YOUR TEAM OR GROUP

In what ways does your team connect with each other? For example, weekly meetings, lunch and learns, social events.

_____

_____

_____

_____

Which methods of connecting are working well?

_____

_____

_____

_____

Which methods of connecting are not working well?

_____

_____

_____

_____

When the group envisions a well-connected team, what does that look, feel, and sound like?

_____

_____

_____

_____

What are two to three things that need to happen to bring your team or group closer together?

_____

_____

_____

_____

Lesson # 32

YOUR BEHAVIOURS

Something I found very useful for understanding myself better was to recognize the various behaviours I gravitate to when I am struggling and the different ones I employ when I am feeling good.

For me, journaling tended to be an activity I did when I was feeling down. I used it to reflect on what was actually going on for me. Then, over the years, I started to journal no matter how I was feeling.

Also, I recognized that when I was going through a period of depression, I would be eating poorly, not exercising, watching more television, and not connecting with friends and family.

Now I can make changes to my behaviour sooner because I recognize the pattern faster.

Here is something I wrote when I was feeling really good.

JOURNAL ENTRY MAY 25, 2007

I feel like the fog has left,

I feel energized again,

I feel excited,

I feel like I have a purpose,

I feel confident,

I feel focused,

I feel like laughing more,

I feel like having fun,

I feel like being silly,

I feel like a meaningful person,

I feel loved,

I feel like me.

EXERCISE FOR YOU

Here is an opportunity for you to reflect on your various behaviours when life is good and also when you are struggling. Spend some time writing about this.

_____

_____

_____

_____

EXERCISE FOR YOUR TEAM OR GROUP

If people are open to it, you can spend some time having the group share their individual answers.

_____

_____

_____

_____

Are there any other behaviours the team observes when the group is struggling or not performing at a high level?

_____

_____

_____

_____

What does the team observe when it is performing high and is well-connected as a group?

_____

_____

_____

_____

How can your team or group ensure the beneficial behaviours occur on a more consistent basis?

_____

_____

_____

_____

Lesson # 33

YOUR FAMILY DYNAMIC

Where we came from can provide a lot of insight into where we are today. During my counselling training at Clearmind International, I had an opportunity to review my family history. The exercise involved examining a variety of perspectives of different generations of my family. I gained perspective in how past generations communicated with each other, their values, their beliefs, the family rules, and so on, and how all these were taught to future generations.

For example, some of the rules in my family were "Turn the lights out when you leave a room" and "Kids should be seen and not heard."

EXERCISE FOR YOU

This journaling exercise can help you gain knowledge about the rules you may still be following in your life unconsciously. These rules may or may not be in line with your values. What lessons were you taught in your family?

What lessons were your parents taught by their parents?

What rules are followed in your family?

_____

_____

_____

_____

Which rules are you still following today?

_____

_____

_____

_____

Are there any rules you are following today that are moving you toward your goal or intention?

_____

_____

_____

_____

EXERCISE FOR YOUR TEAM OR GROUP

If the group is open to it, you can have people share their individual answers for this lesson. This can be an interesting way for the team to really understand where their team members came from.

_____

_____

_____

_____

How can a better understanding of an individual team member's family dynamics help this group move toward success?

_____

_____

_____

_____

What rules are working for the group?

_____

_____

_____

_____

What rules are not working for the group?

_____

_____

_____

_____

What are two or three takeaways the group has learned from this exercise?

_____

_____

_____

_____

Lesson # 34

CONNECT WITH YOURSELF

An important practice I have found value in is connecting with myself. I have done this by listening to inspiring music or going for a walk at a park. When I feel stressed or overwhelmed, I recognize these emotions as signposts telling me to connect with myself.

EXERCISE FOR YOU

What works for you to fully connect with yourself? Write down some things you can do to reconnect with yourself.

_____

_____

_____

_____

Choose one and practise it within twenty-four hours.

_____

_____

_____

EXERCISE FOR YOUR TEAM OR GROUP

You can have team members share what works best for them individually to connect with themselves. Again, this is another way the team can get to know each other better and ultimately bring the team closer together.

_____

_____

_____

_____

How can the team use this information to help the team consistently be successful at moving toward its overall intention?

_____

_____

_____

_____

NOTES

Lesson # 35

YOUR RESPONSE TO CONNECTION

Something I have learned over the years that is quite interesting is how we respond when we connect with ourself and others. The interest in the connection can either grow as well or it can potentially fade.

I know for myself I used to feel very comfortable with people initially and then over time as they got to know me more, I would become more self-conscious.

My journal entry below provides some insight into what happens for me when I am in groups of people. Over the years, I have tended to distance my connection with a group until I know I am safe and can trust the group. In high school, I was very sensitive to name calling and bullying especially in a group environment in which I became the focal point.

JOURNAL ENTRY NOVEMBER 26, 2010

I figured out that I have become very self-conscious of what people think of me when I interact in public. I realized just how affected I was by this in high school.

EXERCISE FOR YOU

How do you respond to connection with yourself and/or other people?

_____

_____

_____

_____

When you spend quiet time with yourself, what happens?

_____

_____

_____

_____

Do you find yourself needing to do something?

_____

_____

_____

_____

Are you comfortable with the silence?

_____

_____

_____

_____

What thoughts start running through your mind?

_____

_____

_____

_____

What is your pattern related to connection when you meet someone for the first time or become part of a team at work or in a sport?

_____

_____

_____

_____

What happens to your connection with a group as time goes on?

_____

_____

_____

_____

EXERCISE FOR YOUR TEAM OR GROUP

You can have your team or group share their individual responses to this exercise, especially to the question related to people's patterns when they first join a team and what happens to the connection over time.

_____

_____

_____

_____

Your team or group has been sharing a lot with each other through these exercises. What are people noticing as far as the group's response to increasing connection?

_____

_____

_____

_____

Is there any resistance to the connection?

_____

_____

_____

_____

If so, in what way?

_____

_____

_____

Why might this be occurring?

_____

_____

_____

_____

How can this group use the resistance to actually bring people together?

_____

_____

_____

_____

Is the group completely open to connecting more and more with each other?

_____

_____

_____

_____

If so, how come?

_____

_____

_____

_____

What is in place to allow this to occur?

_____

_____

_____

_____

What is one action step this group can take to recognize over time how the group is responding to connecting with each other?

_____

_____

_____

_____

Lesson # 36

YOUR BREATH

I still have moments when I catch myself holding my breath or breathing shallowly.

Also, it amazes me how quickly I can forget how sitting and breathing can relax me and open new insights into a struggle I am dealing with.

One breathing exercise I do is counting a hundred breaths. By the time I get to one hundred, I am very relaxed and my stress level is way down.

EXERCISE FOR YOU

Write about what you notice about your breathing this week and any patterns you are aware of.

_____

_____

_____

_____

Do you hold your breath when you are nervous?

_____

_____

_____

_____

Is your chest tight when you are at work or speaking to certain people?

_____

_____

_____

_____

What else do you notice?

_____

_____

_____

_____

EXERCISE FOR YOUR TEAM OR GROUP

This team can share their observations from the individual exercises.

_____

_____

_____

_____

What benefits did the team find from being more aware of their breathing throughout the day?

_____

_____

_____

What can the group do to help encourage team members to spend time being aware of their breathing on a daily basis?

_____

_____

_____

Lesson # 37

REVIEW LESSONS 22 TO 36

I always found it amazing when I would look back on my past journal entries. I would learn so much about myself by reflecting back on where I had come from.

JOURNAL ENTRY APRIL 3, 2005

Having a journal to look back on is an amazing way to review my thoughts, feelings, etc. For the past 4-5 weeks (maybe more) I have been doing lots of thinking, lots of worrying, why do people not like me, why do people not talk to me, why am I so quiet, why do I not feel normal, why do I continually go through periods of highs and lows, am I depressed, am I sick, why does my manager hate me, why do I want to sleep all the time, why do I not feel romantic, why am I worrying about money? I can't remember anything, the future is hard to imagine, I feel lost, I need a hobby, I am so tired, I can do that later, I can't do that, it costs money. How am I going to succeed at work? I want to be a teacher in some way, shape or form.

EXERCISE FOR YOU

Spend some time reviewing the journal entries you have written from the previous lessons in the Connect section of this workbook. What do you notice?

_____

_____

_____

_____

What have you learned about yourself?

_____

_____

_____

_____

What are two simple actions you can take to make changes in your own life based on what you have learned about connection?

_____

_____

_____

_____

EXERCISE FOR YOUR TEAM OR GROUP

If the team is open to it, you can have people share their personal experiences with the exercises in the Engage and Connect sections of the workbook.

_____

_____

_____

_____

What has the team learned about each other?

_____

_____

_____

What are two simple actions the team can take to make connection a priority for its members?

_____

_____

_____

NOTES

NOTES

NOTES

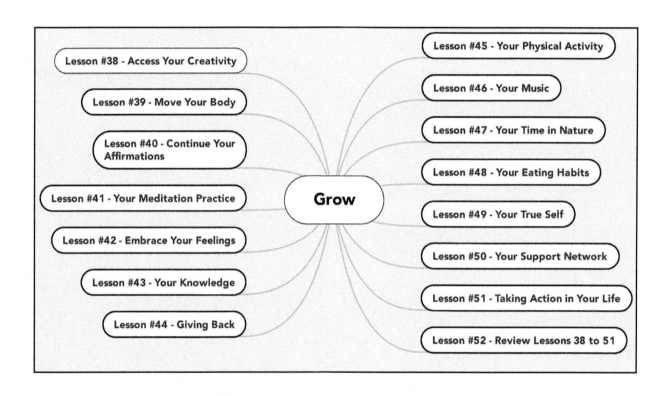

Lesson #38 - Access Your Creativity

Lesson #39 - Move Your Body

Lesson #40 - Continue Your Affirmations

Lesson #41 - Your Meditation Practice

Lesson #42 - Embrace Your Feelings

Lesson #43 - Your Knowledge

Lesson #44 - Giving Back

Grow

Lesson #45 - Your Physical Activity

Lesson #46 - Your Music

Lesson #47 - Your Time in Nature

Lesson #48 - Your Eating Habits

Lesson #49 - Your True Self

Lesson #50 - Your Support Network

Lesson #51 - Taking Action in Your Life

Lesson #52 - Review Lessons 38 to 51

Part 3
GROW

"Unless you try to do something beyond what you have already mastered, you will never grow."
Ralph Waldo Emerson

The definition of "to grow" is "to become larger or greater over a period of time; to increase; to arise or issue as a natural development from an original happening, circumstance, or source."

Congratulations! You have completed thirty-seven lessons. You have completed a lot of work and most likely you have learned a lot about yourself and your team.

The final section of the workbook is called "Grow." In this section, the focus is taking everything you have learned up to this point and finding ways to take action or grow from that learning.

You will be working on lessons in areas related to creativity, health, nature, and support.

This is where you can truly start to move into new areas, ideas, and perspectives. Now is the opportunity to go outside your comfort zone. Enjoy the journey.

Lesson # 38

ACCESS YOUR CREATIVITY

Creativity is a powerful resource to access. It can provide you with insight and direction when you least expect it. Over the years, I gravitated to writing poems to express myself. Here are a couple from different times in my life.

JOURNAL ENTRY MARCH 16, 1998

I'm approaching a fork in the road of life,
The fork we have all seen at least once or twice,
Of course, uncertainty lies behind the one way and security lies behind another,
So what is more important? Or what do I feel is most important?
I've always been shitty at risk-taking,
Always took the easy road,
Using good old common sense,
The thing is that I'm not at the fork yet,
I'm playing the waiting game for something to bring me to the fork,
When I should be gradually approaching the fork on my own,
It's all about controlling one's destiny or achieving a dream,
I'm wanting more control, which is at my control,
The fact that I have recognized this is a great achievement,
Expressing it in words that are getting me to that big old fork in the road.

JOURNAL ENTRY MARCH 18, 2013

The land of the free,
The love of the fire,
The water can break

215

From true love's desire.

Move throughout with ease,
For Heaven can't fall,
Trust in your guidance,
For it's the answer you seek.

Breathe, young wise one,
Feel what's inside,
Your pain, your joy, your past, perhaps?
Nothing brings you truth like the truth of who you are.

EXERCISE FOR YOU

Spend a few minutes writing a poem, a song, a fairy tale, a funny story. Don't think about it too much. Close your eyes for a moment and breathe if needed and just write. It doesn't have to be perfect. It doesn't have to rhyme. All it is is what happens in this moment for you. Just write.

_____

_____

_____

_____

EXERCISE FOR YOUR TEAM OR GROUP

You can have people share their creative talents with the group if people are open to it.

_____

_____

_____

_____

How can this team or group utilize the creativity of its members to continue growing to a new level of performance?

_____

_____

_____

What is one creative endeavour this team or group can commit to doing within the next week?

_____

_____

_____

Lesson # 39

MOVE YOUR BODY

Movement is all around us. The blood in our bodies needs to move to keep us alive. There is a flow to life. Take steps no matter the size to get you to the experience you truly want to have.

If you hear about a book, buy it. If you see an event or course that can help you, look into it. Journal, Read, Feel, Learn, Meditate, Breathe, Observe, Connect.

EXERCISE FOR YOU

Move your body. Dance. Jump. Walk. Skip. Sway. Now, give yourself permission to move. Give it a try and notice what happens. Write about what you noticed.

_____

_____

_____

EXERCISE FOR YOUR TEAM OR GROUP

People can share with the group about their experience of moving if they choose.

_____

_____

_____

_____

How can your group use movement to help with its performance? This would be especially important if team members are sitting at a desk throughout the day.

_____

_____

_____

_____

NOTES

Lesson # 40

CONTINUE YOUR AFFIRMATIONS

Positive affirmations are so powerful. They can train your mind to focus on the good in your life versus your fears. Here are some affirmations I have used in the past.

"Love" [Repeat this word a hundred times.]

"I have a purpose to positively impact the world."

"I am strong & confident."

"I can accomplish anything I desire."

"I am surrounded by positive people in my life."

EXERCISE FOR YOU

Choose one affirmation to say to yourself daily. You can use one you created from lesson twenty-five or something else. You can write it somewhere where you will see it every day such as posted on your bathroom mirror or beside your desk.

_____

_____

_____

_____

Be aware of how you feel as you use your affirmation. You can write about this in your journal.

_____

_____

_____

Over time, you can decide if you would like to add additional affirmations.

_____

_____

_____

_____

EXERCISE FOR YOUR TEAM OR GROUP

You can have people share their individual affirmations with the group if people are open to it.

_____

_____

_____

_____

How can the group embrace everyone's affirmations to help the collective group grow and evolve?

_____

_____

_____

_____

Is there an affirmation that speaks to the entire group? Can it be put in a place where everyone can see it? Write that affirmation here.

_____

_____

_____

Lesson # 41

YOUR MEDITATION PRACTICE

The universe continues to send me information, events, books, audio recordings, and more about meditation. I have experienced benefits from it and at the same time I am still learning how to make it a regular activity.

EXERCISE FOR YOU

Learn about the practice of meditating and try it. For the next week, sit for one minute or an amount of time you are comfortable with and focus only on your breath. What do you notice? Journal about your experience.

_____

_____

_____

_____

EXERCISE FOR YOUR TEAM OR GROUP

People can share their meditation experience with the group.

_____

_____

_____

_____

Can daily meditation help this group?

_____

_____

_____

_____

If so, how?

_____

_____

_____

_____

What can the group do to incorporate daily meditation as an advantageous practice?

_____

_____

_____

_____

Lesson # 42

EMBRACE YOUR FEELINGS

For many years, being aware of my feeling always "felt" challenging for me. I kept most of my feelings inside and locked away. If you can find ways to become more aware of your feelings, you can bring some great energy into your life. I believe the idea is to come to a place where all feelings are welcome. No judgements, guilt, or shame. Feelings are part of us and can bring us so much when we give ourselves the chance to embrace them.

EXERCISE FOR YOU

One thing you can do throughout the day is stop for a moment and ask yourself how you are feeling in this moment. Write it down. You can write anything related to it.

_____

_____

_____

_____

You may not be feeling anything. You can write about that.

_____

_____

_____

_____

You may be feeling a variety of things—you can write about all of them.

_____

_____

_____

EXERCISE FOR YOUR TEAM OR GROUP

You can have the team share their experience with being aware of their feelings on a daily basis.

_____

_____

_____

_____

What themes did the group notice when people shared their experiences of noticing their feelings?

_____

_____

_____

_____

Were others feeling the same way?

_____

_____

_____

_____

What similarities does the team notice about what everyone experienced?

_____

_____

_____

_____

How can this group use this exercise to help everyone on the team grow to their full potential?

_____

_____

_____

_____

Lesson # 43

YOUR KNOWLEDGE

Reading books is something I have done since I was young. I have always enjoyed it. I read a lot of books by Stephen King throughout my high school years. Reading has helped me with creativity and visualization.

When I hit my late twenties and early thirties, I started to read more self-help books.

When I reflect back, it is quite amazing how certain books seemed to find me at specific times in my life.

The Feeling Good Handbook by David D. Burns became an ongoing resource for me when I was trying to better understand my depression.

Below are some of books I have read over the years.

Angel Therapy Handbook, The by Doreen Virtue

Attractor Factor, The by Joe Vitale

Awakened Wisdom by Patrick J. Ryan

Bible, The

Case for Christ, The by Lee Strobel

Courage of Magic Johnson, The by Peter F. Pascarelli

Course in Miracles, A scribed by Helen Schucman with William Thetford

Don't Sweat the Small Stuff by Richard Carlson, PhD

Drive by Daniel H. Pink

Dying to Be Me by Anita Moorjani

Extraordinary Relationships by Roberta M. Gilbert, MD

Feeling Good Handbook, The by David D. Burns, MD

For One More Day by Mitch Albom

Four Agreements, The by Don Miguel Ruiz

Greatest Salesman in the World , The by Og Mandino

Illuminata by Marianne Williamson

Jonathan Livingston Seagull by Richard Bach

Law of Attraction by Michael J. Losier

Lightworkers Way, The by Doreen Virtue

Little Book of Life by Neale Donald Walsch

Living the Wisdom of the Tao by Dr. Wayne Dyer

Men Are from Mars, Women Are from Venus by John Gray

My Spiritual Journey by the 14th Dalai Lama

Power of Now, The by Eckhart Tolle

Purpose Driven Life, The by Rick Warren

Return to Love, A by Marianne Williamson

Rich Dad, Poor Dad by Robert Kiyosaki and Sharon Lechter

Richest Man in Babylon, The by George S. Clason

Spiritual Selling by Joe Nunziata

Success Principles, The by Jack Canfield and Janet Switzer

System for Soul Memory, The by Susan Kerr

Tuesdays with Morrie by Mitch Albom

What Color Is Your Parachute? by Richard Nelson Bolles

When Everything Changes, Change Everything by Neale Donald Walsch

Why Walk When You Can Fly? by Isha Judd

EXERCISE FOR YOU

Have any of the books you have read made an impact on your life? If so, spend some time reflecting and writing about this. List some of them here.

_____

_____

_____

_____

Use the space below to list the learnings you want to remember from the book(s) you are currently reading.

_____

_____

_____

_____

Go on an adventure to your local bookstore and spend some time in the self-help section. See if you are drawn to any particular books. Use the space below to list the books you are interested in.

_____

_____

_____

_____

EXERCISE FOR YOUR TEAM OR GROUP

You can have the team share which books or resources have made a huge impact on their life.

_____

_____

_____

_____

How does the team want to use books or other resources to help this group enhance its knowledge and skills?

_____

_____

_____

_____

NOTES

Lesson # 44

GIVING BACK

A powerful way to become more engaged in your life and continue your growth is to help someone in need. You can volunteer at a local charity, offer to buy a coffee for a homeless person, or give away clothes or other belongings to a local organization.

EXERCISE FOR YOU

Find someone you can help this week. It is important to take action based on your heart versus your head. Spend some more time breathing and allowing the right person or organization to present themselves. Also, the way you can help may not be what you expect. Take some time to write about your experience here.

_____

_____

_____

_____

EXERCISE FOR YOUR TEAM OR GROUP

You can have the members of your group share their individual experiences with helping someone this week.

_____

_____

_____

_____

How can this group give back to the community in some way? You may want to review the group's values from lesson twenty-four and find something that is in line with the overall values of the group.

_____

_____

_____

_____

NOTES

Lesson # 45

YOUR PHYSICAL ACTIVITY

Over the years, walking, running, biking, hiking, basketball, and volleyball have worked well for me. When I was feeling really low, it would take all my energy to just go for a short walk. I would start small and work up from there. I seem to have gotten into the habit of tracking the times I exercise. Today, there are some great app's that can help with this versus the good old excel spreadsheet I used to use.

The key thing for me when it comes to exercising is it helps clear my head of all the negative self-talk. Also, I find I can end up receiving a variety of new creative ideas I had never thought of before.

EXERCISE FOR YOU

What are you already doing or what can you start to do in a simple way to embrace exercise in your life? Write down these ways here.

_____

_____

_____

_____

Start with the simplest thing you can do for sure. What is it?

_____

_____

_____

_____

How can you commit to making exercise a priority in your life?

_____

_____

_____

_____

EXERCISE FOR YOUR TEAM OR GROUP

Have the group spend some time sharing how they embrace exercise in their life.

_____

_____

_____

_____

What ways can the team embrace exercise at work, such as during a break or lunch hour?

_____

_____

_____

What is one commitment the team can make with regard to exercising more?

_____

_____

_____

_____

Lesson # 46

YOUR MUSIC

Over the years, I have been writing about key stories from my life. As part of this writing, I realized how music has had such a positive impact on my life. For me, I really enjoy listening to a variety of types of music. Music energizes me. It empowers me. It motivates me. It relaxes me. It helps me meditate. It helps me focus. It brings joy and fun into my life. I love singing in the car and playing music at home and dancing like no one else is watching. I have found I have shifted my music interest to genres that have lyrics with positive—even inspirational—messages.

EXERCISE FOR YOU

How has music been part of your life?

_____

_____

_____

_____

What positive experiences have you had with music?

_____

_____

_____

_____

If you listen to or perform music regularly, what types of music do you like?

_____

_____

_____

_____

What are the lyrics of the songs you like?

_____

_____

_____

_____

Are the lyrics consistent with your values and beliefs?

_____

_____

_____

_____

Are there types of music that help you relax, give you energy, or clear your head? Spend some time listening to music and write down what you notice.

_____

_____

_____

_____

If you don't listen to music regularly, what are some ways music could help you with your own personal growth?

_____

_____

_____

_____

EXERCISE FOR YOUR TEAM OR GROUP

Spend some time having the group share their personal experiences about music.

_____

_____

_____

_____

What did the team learn from each other from sharing this?

_____

_____

_____

_____

How can this group use music to help the team be more productive, connect better, and ultimately grow? Come up with three specific ways.

_____

_____

_____

_____

How can the group incorporate these specific ways on a regular basis?

_____

_____

_____

_____

Lesson # 47

YOUR TIME IN NATURE

I have found some great benefits of getting out in nature. I am a morning person and I really enjoy a walk, a run, or a bike ride through a park or along a beach. This is another great way to clear your mind and ground yourself in the power within you.

EXERCISE FOR YOU

What ways do you spend time in nature currently?

_____

_____

_____

_____

How can you spend more time in nature in your life if you know it can benefit you?

_____

_____

_____

_____

Where is somewhere close to you that you could visit this week? Bring your journal along and write about your experience. Commit to spending time in nature within twenty-four hours.

_____

_____

_____

_____

EXERCISE FOR YOUR TEAM OR GROUP

You can have the team share their experience(s) related to spending time in nature.

_____

_____

_____

_____

What benefits could this group receive from spending more time in nature?

_____

_____

_____

What can this group do to help ensure time spent in nature is a regular habit?

_____

_____

_____

_____

Lesson # 48

YOUR EATING HABITS

I am no expert at this. I am not going to tell you that I am eating only organic foods. What I have done is started to gradually make smarter food choices.

For me, I used to eat a lot of pasta and carbs. It was my go-to meal choice. I found myself always tired with no energy to do very much. I made a choice to increase my water consumption every day. I have stomach issues with IBS (irritable bowel syndrome) and a potential gluten issue, so I reduced the amount of milk and gluten I consume. The one thing I have noticed is my mind is a lot clearer and if I have a low period, it doesn't last as long. I am able to come out of it faster.

EXERCISE FOR YOU

A great exercise is to record the food you eat each day for a few weeks to get really clear as to what types of foods you are eating regularly. Then you can determine whether you need to make any changes to your diet.

_____

_____

_____

_____

What do you experience when you eat junk food, sweets, snacks?

_____

_____

_____

_____

What do you experience when you eat healthier foods?

_____

_____

_____

_____

What steps can you take to recognize ways to make healthier eating choices?

_____

_____

_____

_____

EXERCISE FOR YOUR TEAM OR GROUP

If people are open to it, you can have the team share their individual answers.

_____

_____

_____

_____

What are the typical foods the team orders for meetings and events?

_____

_____

_____

_____

Are there healthy food choices the team can make for future team meetings and events?

_____

_____

_____

_____

Lesson # 49

YOUR TRUE SELF

I always thought the goal was to be constantly happy. Here is a journal entry of mine about this when I was still in school. I was struggling with focusing on being happy when at the time I really wasn't. This was at a time when I was questioning a lot about myself and my future.

JOURNAL ENTRY FROM 2014

This is something I wrote in 2014 during my second year of counsellor training. I wrote it after doing a meditation exercise.

Aaron, you are so strong. You are doing everything exactly as you are. Trust your heart, your instincts, that feeling of love inside you. It is guiding you to love. You know exactly what you need to do. Your ego is someone you can love. Your ego is getting louder because you have always used it for guidance. It doesn't know what to do when you don't listen so it gets louder. Run, meditate, breathe, do whatever you need to do to calm your body so you can access your true self. Grandpa loves you. He is with you every step of the way. He uses the radio to communicate. He is there if you need him. Grandpa loves you. I love you, Aaron. I love you. Aaron, love yourself every day in some way. Say the words. Say them & mean them. Feel them in your heart. Love yourself always no matter what. You matter, Aaron. You matter so much to the world & your family. Move based on love. If you are moving for another reason it is not true to you. You know what to be. You know how to evolve. You are evolving. Everything is coming together. Be patient. Embrace patience. Receive wisdom. Experience calm & be free. Breathe, Aaron. It is the simplest & easiest thing you can do every day. Focus on as many breaths as you can. You are beautiful.

You are innocent. You are innocent. You matter. You are love. You are love. I will keep saying this. If you get stuck in the future focus on you in the future & where you are headed. Love is where you are headed. You are so there right now. Express love to others & watch what happens. Watch, Aaron, & feel it. Be present. Be present. Learn to be present.

EXERCISE FOR YOU

Find a quiet place to sit and breathe for a period of time you are comfortable with. Have this workbook and a pen with you. Focus on accessing your true self, your Self whose focus is on compassion, curiosity, joy, love, and peace.

_____

_____

_____

_____

After you have sat in silence for a period of time, start to write from the perspective of your true self. Write continuously without pausing or stopping. Write whatever messages come to you and do this for two minutes without stopping.

_____

_____

_____

_____

What did you notice when doing this exercise?

_____

_____

_____

_____

What did you learn about yourself during this exercise?

_____

_____

_____

_____

What is your true self guiding you to do or be?

_____

_____

_____

_____

EXERCISE FOR YOUR TEAM OR GROUP

If people are open to it, you can have them share what they wrote from the perspective of their true self.

_____

_____

_____

_____

What does the group notice from the sharing?

_____

_____

_____

Are there any themes or similarities among the group?

_____

_____

_____

_____

How can this group use what has been learned about everyone's true self to help the team grow and evolve?

_____

_____

_____

_____

NOTES

Lesson # 50

YOUR SUPPORT NETWORK

At times it may not feel like this; however, support is all around you. I know when I was experiencing depression, I had challenges finding it. Support can be a book, a video, a friend, a loved one, a doctor, a teacher, a therapist, a coach, a support group, and more.

There are resources in your own community to help you with whatever struggle you are facing, no matter how scary it is. If that resource isn't in your community, there are people who can help you find the help you need.

Be open to support when you are struggling. Be open to support when you are feeling amazing. Support is all about staying connected to another person. Connection with ourselves is foundational; connection with others takes us to new heights and allows us to grow.

EXERCISE FOR YOU

What is your relationship with support?

_____

_____

_____

_____

Do you initially avoid asking for help?

_____

_____

_____

_____

If so, how come?

_____

_____

_____

_____

Do you have lots of support and are not getting what you need from it?

_____

_____

_____

_____

Do you tend not to ask for support?

_____

_____

_____

_____

Who makes up your support network?

_____

_____

_____

_____

What are some ways you can obtain additional support if needed?

_____

_____

_____

_____

EXERCISE FOR YOUR TEAM OR GROUP

How does this team support each other?

_____

_____

_____

_____

What is working?

_____

_____

_____

_____

What are the barriers?

_____

_____

_____

_____

How can this group obtain the support it requires to reach its goal or intention?

_____

_____

_____

_____

What has the group learned from each other through this workbook that can help with obtaining support when need?

_____

_____

_____

_____

Lesson # 51

TAKING ACTION IN YOUR LIFE

On reading these journal entries below, I find them amazing. I can now see how I was taking steps to make my passion a reality. I started with writing it out and then creating a plan to make it all come together.

JOURNAL ENTRY MAY 29, 2010

It is all about taking action. There is a huge need to help people to start taking action.

JOURNAL ENTRY AUGUST 12, 2010

What do you want to take action on?
exercise—have a regular schedule
I want to generate income from my website
write a book
create a training program
create a coaching program
buy a house in 2011
feel present with my family and friends
build a consistent referral system
have extra $ to pay off debt
strengthen my mind
be unafraid of doing certain things
be a better communicator
How would I take action on each item if I had the power to do so?
do daily exercises to strengthen my mind and reduce my limiting fears—Isha system
need to commit to a business plan at my current job and implement it in order to generate the

income I require to try other things

meditate daily

pick 4 days a week to exercise for a minimum of 30 minutes

write & read every chance I get

create a sales process and follow it

What would I do for a career if it were in my power to change tomorrow?

write books, have videos, and create software that help a special niche strengthen their mind

have a home office or a small one close to home

spend my days coaching, doing video training live online

create a foundation whose purpose is to provide programs to youth to strengthen their minds

EXERCISE FOR YOU

What are three attainable steps you can take to become more engaged and connected so as to grow?

_____

_____

_____

_____

EXERCISE FOR YOUR TEAM OR GROUP

What are three attainable steps you can take to become more engaged and connected to obtain growth?

_____

_____

_____

_____

Lesson # 52

REVIEW LESSONS 38 TO 51

Congratulations, you have made it to the final lesson. Way to go! I can imagine you have learned a lot by completing all the lessons.

Here is another opportunity for you to spend some quality time reading through your journal entries from the Grow section of the workbook.

EXERCISE FOR YOU

Spend some time reviewing the journal entries you have written from the previous lessons in the Grow section of this workbook. What do you notice?

_____

_____

_____

_____

What have you learned about yourself?

_____

_____

_____

What are two simple actions you can take to make changes in your own life based on what you have learned about growth?

EXERCISE FOR YOUR TEAM OR GROUP

If the team is open to it, you can have people share their personal experiences with the exercises in the Grow section of this workbook.

_____

_____

_____

_____

What has the team learned about each other?

_____

_____

_____

_____

What are two simple actions the team can take to make growth a priority for this group?

_____

_____

_____

_____

NOTES

NOTES

ABOUT THE AUTHOR

Aaron's own life journey has been focused on personal and professional growth.

As a teenager and young adult, he silently struggled with low self-esteem and depression. For a long time, he felt disconnected from who he was and from how to express his true self to his friends, family, and coworkers.

Over twenty years of journaling—and taking additional steps to ultimately show compassion and love for himself—enabled him to gain a sense of awareness of who he is and the amazing gifts he can bring to the world.

His passion is to guide individuals, corporate teams and organizations to the heart of what truly matters to them.

He is able to bring his passion to others through his company, Engage Coaching Group, as a Registered Therapeutic Counsellor, an author, a coach, and a teacher. Aaron has over fifteen years of combined business development experience in the financial services and technology industries. He holds a Diploma in Transpersonal Counselling Psychology from Clearmind International Institute and a Bachelor of Business Administration from Simon Fraser University with a major in Human Resource Management.

Aaron was born in Burnaby, British Columbia (BC), Canada and he spent the majority of his childhood in Williams Lake, BC. He is a father, son, husband, friend, and self-loving man. He currently lives in Langley, BC, Canada, with his wife Farrah and two sons.

AUTHOR'S SERVICES

Engage Coaching Group focuses on providing continuous support to help you and your team ignite your passion and bring all of yourself to your life and your work. Our focus is to guide individuals, corporate teams, and organizations to the heart of what truly matters to them.

I hope you found this workbook helpful in your life and for your team. If you did and you would like to receive more help, go to EngageCoachingGroup.com, where more support is available to you in the form of

- Blog articles
- Online programs
- One-on-one coaching
- One-on-one counselling

Also, I would love to hear how this book has impacted your life, your team, and your organization.

Aaron would love to hear about your experience with completing the 52 lessons.
You can reach him via email at info@EngageCoachingGroup.com or by phone at 604-731-7933.

Interact with others who are reading this book at:
www.facebook.com/groups/engageconnectgrow/

CPSIA information can be obtained
at www.ICGtesting.com
Printed in the USA
LVOW04s0718010917

547223LV00002B/3/P